THE
BLUE
PRINT

Ade O...

∠ Jeremiah 29:11 >

The BLUE PRINT

DISCOVER WHAT GOD HAS IN STORE FOR YOUR LIFE

ROBERT PARK

Mill City Press
Minneapolis, MN

Mill City Press, Inc.
322 First Avenue N, 5th floor
Minneapolis, MN 55401
612.455.2293
www.millcitypublishing.com

ISBN-13: 978-1-63413-076-9
LCCN: 2014916256

Book Design by Sophie Chi

Printed in the United States of America

Dedication

————◆————

THIS BOOK IS DEDICATED TO MY FRIEND Jae Kim (1952–2013). Jae's unwavering love and support for me and my ministry, as well as his commitment to the kingdom of God, left an indelible impression on my life. Your sudden departure is still a shock to us all, but we look forward to our reunion in heaven.

To my wife, Susan, who through all tribulations has always stood by me, believed in me, and given me her very best.

To Jeanna and Timothy and our daughter-in-law, Sugie, you are my precious jewels.

And to the members of New Life Baptist Church, your faith, love, and support have been more than I could hope for.

Contents

— • —

CONTENTS

Introduction

————•————

YOU'VE PROBABLY SEEN A BLUEPRINT. THE white lines drawn on special blue paper depict buildings or other structures. Simply put, a blueprint is a plan for construction or assembly.

I once had an opportunity to be involved in a huge building project. We didn't start by throwing together two-by-fours; neither did we guess how many drywall boards we'd need. Before lifting a hammer, we hired an architect to design the building. He asked us the size of the building, its purpose, what features were necessary, where it would be located, and many other questions. From our answers, he discerned exactly what we wanted and needed. Once we agreed on the general schematics, he drew the plans. They included several pages of blueprints detailing every aspect of the building: structure, mechanical, plumbing, electrical, and more, right down to the landscaping. With the help of computer technology, he even calculated the total number of nails and screws we would need to build the structure.

This stage of the process (before any building is done) can cost up to 25 percent of a project's total budget. Yet it is a crucial phase of the undertaking. If the contractors don't follow the blueprints, the building can fall apart at any point, causing terrible destruction, even fatalities.

At a particularly low point of my life, I felt that all was against me. No matter how hard I tried to make a living or be a good son, father, and husband, I perceived myself as a failure. All my plans seemed to come apart at the seams. I questioned my career choice, my abilities . . . everything, including God. I whined to Him about the injustices, discrimination, and unfairness aimed at me. But God wasn't the only one to hear my complaints.

I arrived home from work after an exceptionally discouraging day and started in with my wife, Sue. At the end of my self-pitying tirade, I shook my head and said, "I want to just give up."

Maybe today you are where I was that day, ready to give up because your plans have backfired, crashed, and burned. No doubt you've experienced something so unfair it made you question whether every choice you'd ever made was wrong. Maybe the person who should have been protecting you betrayed you instead, and so you wonder if all your friends are lining up to stab you in the back. Your world feels topsy-turvy. Your life is a smoldering heap of shattered plans.

Let me share the wisdom of my wife that day.

Sue took my hand, looked me in the eyes, and said, "The worst thing you can do is give up. I don't think God has given up on you. You are only accepting defeat when you react the way you do."

And then she opened her Bible to Jeremiah 29:11 and read it to me: "'For I know the plans I have for you,' declares the LORD, "plans to prosper you and not to harm you, plans to give you hope and a future.'"

The truth of Jeremiah's words opened up for me a panoramic view of life. Even if my plans lay in shards, God's plan remained intact. His was an overarching plan to give me hope and a future. He wanted good things for me, and I could count on Him for that. As I thought about it, I realized that, at best, I had based my plans on shallow desires: wealth, power, position. They had to be torn down to make way for God's far better plans for my life.

God's grace, goodness, and love are toward His people. If His plan is for our welfare, hope, and a future, then we are assured that whatever He has in mind for us is good and won't harm us.

The Blueprint is my journey. You'll read of my plans and how I worked them. Then you'll see how God replaced my inferior, short-sighted, selfish ideas with His much-improved and far-reaching ones. The time between my plans falling apart and His taking root was, shall we say, rocky. But that's how it is when one building is imploded to make way for the new and improved one. A big mess and a great deal of debris must be gathered and hauled away before the new structure is built.

His plan in my life has grown and blossomed in ways I could never have imagined. I'll share with you how it helped me become an instrument for bringing His plan, hope, and a future to others, including His people in Cuba.

The Master Architect is great, and His plan intertwines us with one another in a magnificent fashion only He could devise.

Chapter One

———◆———

SHAKY BEGINNINGS

M Y MOTHER, HEEOK, WAS THE SECOND daughter of the Park family. They lived in Youngdong, a town in central Korea, about 150 miles south of Seoul. As a child she excelled in her studies, graduating from high school as class valedictorian. Despite the cultural barriers preventing girls from getting an education in those days, my grandfather sent my mother to China to attend college.

At the tender age of eighteen, Heeok entered the pre-med program at Beijing University. While there she lived with her sister and brother-in-law, a pharmacologist who also worked in research as an exchange professor. Tall and handsome, he caught the eye of many women and broke his wife's heart with repeated infidelity.

One day he arranged for his wife to be out of the

house for several hours, leaving my mother there alone. When he returned home from work, he raped Mom. But that was only the beginning. Using threats of revealing the incident to the family, which would bring great dishonor to them and shame on my mother, he continued to subjugate her sexually.

Then the inevitable happened—she became pregnant. Not knowing where else to turn, she confessed everything to her sister. Rather than console and help my mother, my aunt became enraged and kicked her out of the house.

Alone and scared in a foreign county, my shamed mother drifted to what was then Manchuria, where she found a doctor who performed an abortion.

With the announcement that World War II had ended, liberating Korea from Japanese rule, also came the life-changing news that Heeok's father had died. My mother headed home, great sadness and loss— of her promising future, her child, and her father— weighing her down.

During the war, my grandfather, Geun-Ha Park, ran a local branch of a major newspaper by day. By night he devoted his time and resources to the resistance movement against Japanese occupation. Using his home as base, he determined the movement's objectives and planned their activities. He recruited and trained new participants, and he directly engaged the enemy. When he died, he left the family penniless, having drained his reserves to finance the resistance movement.

In less than a year, my mother's formerly hope-filled life had spiraled out of control. Once she had envisioned returning home with a diploma and a bright future, but now she had nothing but shame and hopelessness. Yet she could not tell her family of the abuse she'd suffered from her brother-in-law. To do so would disgrace the family and make life unbearable for her.

My mother looked for work, but there were no jobs for a Korean woman after the war. The one slice of optimism seemed to come in the form of the American troops who had arrived as part of the UN Advisory Team, dispatched to Korea to help prevent a civil war. Mother had learned English in high school, so she tried to get work as a translator, but the hours were sporadic and too few to make a living. She struggled to survive.

She had access to the PX store on the US military base. So she bought watches, cameras, purses, etc., there as she could and then traded those items on the black market for food and clothing and sometimes a little money. This only added to her already heavy load of humiliation. She felt violated and filthy, yet she concluded that moral values had no importance or place in her life. Loneliness and hunger drove her on.

In one of her encounters with the Americans, she met a young Army captain from Philadelphia, Robert Goosewell (my mother was not certain of the spelling), who affirmed his love for her. They set up housekeeping in a small home in Pildong near Mount Namsan in central Seoul. It wasn't long before she became pregnant with me. I was born in 1949. My father seemed very pleased with his son and named me Robert, after himself. I could not take his last name, because to register my birth required a Korean father. So Mother registered me as her brother's son.

My mother's life seemed to change for the better. It seemed brighter and more hopeful. She was blessed with a son, a man who loved her, and a comfortable place to live. But within a year, my father received orders to return to the United States. One evening, shortly before he was to leave, he made a confession to my mother. He was married.

He promised that he would not abandon us because he felt morally responsible for us. He said he'd divorce his wife then bring my mother and me to the United States. Korea was not a good place to raise me, he said. I should be raised in America. So with that promise in May 1950, my father left Korea.

Neither my mother nor I ever saw him again.

One month later, on June 25, 1950, North Korea invaded the South. Once again my country of birth was catapulted into war.

With my father by her side, Heeok felt settled in life. She had the financial freedom to help support her destitute mother and other relatives. But with my father's exodus and the advent of war, her all-too-brief freedom came to a screeching halt.

Now she had to think not only of her own safety and well-being but also mine. She evacuated Seoul relatively early by crossing the Han River, which bisected the city north and south. As the US and South Korean militaries retreated, they bombed the two lone bridges to slow the rapidly advancing Communist troops. The only way to cross the river now was by boat.

When Mother and I arrived on the southern bank of the river, she frantically searched for her mother and sister. She was certain they had crossed in a separate boat, yet she found no sign of them.

Panic filled the fleeing populace. Clearly, their only thought was to run to safety. But my mother determined to find her loved ones. She asked everyone she encountered if they'd seen them. Many ignored her, intent on their own families' well-being. Others brushed her aside. Those who responded said that they hadn't seen the women and continued their trek. Surrounded by the frenzied masses, my mother fought to control her rising alarm and fear for her mother and sister.

She eventually concluded that her loved ones had been unable to cross the river. With bombs blasting and bullets flying, she had no time to hesitate. She had to go back for them.

Fighting against the crowds fleeing the enemy, she reached the river's edge. It wasn't hard to find a boat going to the northern side. Only the brave but greedy boat owners were still crossing to pick up more passengers. By the time my mother and I landed on the sandy beach of the north side, our fate slammed into her. Red flags pitched in the sand dunes fluttered in the breeze. Young Communist soldiers stood guard along the bank. One soldier held a megaphone to his mouth and blurted, "Go back to your homes. You have nothing to worry about. You will be safe in your homes. You are now liberated. Return to your homes."

Many South Koreans welcomed the Communist military. Soldiers and sympathizers danced in the street, joyously welcoming the new regime.

Liberated? Mom felt anything but. Yet what could she do? With me tied to her back, she trudged home. As she entered the house, she startled to see the young man who had rented one of her rooms. He'd disappeared just a few days prior to the fighting. She eyed him warily, for he now wore the uniform of the North Korean army.

He grinned as if he'd accomplished the evacuation

on his own. "Missus, it has finally happened. We are liberating our country!"

She stood in stunned silence, the shock having robbed her of clear thinking.

He continued. "You should go to Pyongyang, where it is much safer. I will arrange the transportation for you. You and Robert should be well cared for. I have to go now, because my unit is advancing farther south."

She learned that while he'd been a tenant in her home, he'd been spying for North Korea. She felt betrayed by him, hating that she had housed a Communist spy. But she couldn't waste time dwelling on that, for she knew what was at stake. She would have to shift into survival mode.

The Communists controlling the city didn't waste any time cleansing the area of "agents of American imperialists." First they searched for anyone who had anything to do with the Americans or the South Korean government. Then they wasted no time in setting up People's Courts, one of which was held in the playground of the nearby elementary school. Of course, "court" was just a pretense. There was no "innocent until proven guilty." Enemies of the party, be they politicians, police officers, Christians, or rightists, were all guilty. Over the loudspeaker that echoed throughout our neighborhood, Mom heard the charges read, quickly followed by the crack of a rifle shot. Her baby with hazel eyes and light brown hair was sure proof of "American imperialism" and warranted speedy public execution of both of us.

Mother's life had once again turned upside down. Like a mantra that played over and over in her head, she moaned, "Where is my baby's dad?"

She prayed for protection to whatever god might be available. She prayed the soldiers would never come to her house. She prayed the soldiers wouldn't notice me, her light-complexioned baby.

Outbreaks of measles and dysentery were common. I was constantly draining with diarrhea, and Mother feared I might die of dehydration. Our next-door neighbor suggested feeding me *saewujyut* (pickled and fermented baby shrimps). But where disease was abundant, food was scarce and medicine nonexistent. When the bombings stopped, impromptu outdoor markets opened. If you had money, you could buy a little barley and a few other necessities. Rice was no longer available, because it had all been seized for the soldiers. Determined to do what she could to keep me alive, my mother decided to go to the marketplace, hoping it would be open and that she could find the life-saving concoction.

Of course, she couldn't bring me, because my American features would mean certain death for both of us. So Mother took me to the neighbor's house. The kind woman had nine daughters, who were overjoyed that I would be left in their charge. They took me to their basement, where we hid while my mother went to the market.

When she was about a hundred yards from the house, Mother felt an overwhelming intuition that she should not leave me with the neighbor. It made no sense, and it would be dangerous to take me with her. She tried to shake off the feeling, but it nagged at her. Finally, she could no longer fight her maternal instinct and went back for me.

Our neighbor warned Mother of the danger of taking me out in public. "They will kill Robert and you too, Heeok. Please, do not do this. He will be much safer if you leave him here with us."

"If I die, I will die with my baby. We will not be separated."

The girls protested violently, because they feared for our lives.

But Mother would do it her way. "No one is to argue with me about my baby."

And with that final word, she put me on her back and wrapped a blanket over me to hide me. I don't remember the incident, which is a good thing, because being bound to her and completely covered in the ninety-degree heat with August's 96 percent humidity was nothing short of suffocating. But to my mother, this was a small burden to bear if she could find the medicine to heal me.

When she was barely halfway to the marketplace, she heard the eerie but all too familiar high-pitched whistle of an incoming bomb. She ran and jumped into the ditch right before the thunderous explosion shook the ground like a violent earthquake, sending a shock wave over her. At first she feared the bomb had dropped on her, for the air became thick with dirt and debris. She waited, holding her breath. A vacuum of silence followed.

She made a mental check of herself, thankful to be whole and uninjured. My squirming indicated that I, too, was unhurt. When the dust cleared, she lifted her head and peered over the edge of the ditch.

A new fear now clutched her heart. She gazed toward our house, but all she saw was a heap of rubble engulfed in flames. She bolted toward the house, fighting through the crowd of panicked people running in all directions. She slowed as she drew closer. The horror that met her eyes robbed the strength from her legs, and she crumpled to the ground. The house with the nine daughters had received the full fury of the bomb. Nothing—and nobody—remained.

I would have died had Mom not listened to her intuition.

Or was it the voice of God speaking to her?

Chapter Two

———◆———

SURVIVAL

OTHER THAN THE TERRORIST ATTACK ON September 11, 2001, war has not been fought on United States soil for 150 years; therefore, most US citizens do not know what it's like to live in a war zone. A typical day for most American families might include waking up to a hearty breakfast before getting the kids off to school, after which we jump into our cars and head straight to work. At the close of a productive day, we stop by the grocery store on the way home and buy whatever suits our cravings for dinner. We help the kids with their homework then relax in front of the TV before calling it a night and dropping into our comfortable beds. Our days are fairly predictable.

When you live in a war zone, one thought dominates your entire day: survival. This became my mother's life. She didn't consider what she would do tomorrow. Today, this minute, was her only concern. Finding food and water, as well as protecting herself and me, became her full-time job. Her fears of becoming collateral damage, like her neighbors, accompanied her day and night.

My dysentery slowly cleared up, which was a huge relief for Mom. But her biggest fear remained: being caught and executed for collusion with American imperialists, of which I was glaring proof. On two occasions, soldiers came to our house. Adolescents, no older than fifteen or sixteen, they looked like boys playing soldiers, because the rifles hanging on their slight shoulders nearly touched the ground. Their young ages made them careless and gullible. On seeing their approach, Mom would hide me in the closet or in the bathroom then either divert their attention to something else or tell them stories to make them believe nothing was amiss. She called me a good baby for knowing when not to cry.

Fortunately, Mother had some money with which to buy food. When that ran low, she used her valuables, such as a camera, a Swiss watch, and jewelry my dad had bought her, to barter for food.

One question never veered far from Mom's thoughts: Was her mother still alive somewhere?

After miraculously surviving three months that felt like an eternity, my mother began to notice soldiers retreating from the fronts farther south. Though she didn't know a lot about war strategy, she noted that these men were not part of any cohesive unit. Word around the neighborhood was that these soldiers had abandoned their companies. They wore ragged clothes and lacked weapons, but they were loaded with fury and violence. More than one didn't hesitate to use sharpened bamboo sticks to kill anyone who stood in their way.

As was her habit, Mom arose early each morning. One particular morning she sensed a difference in the air. She immediately thought that her mother-radar was going off again and that she should hide me.

Just as she turned to go back inside, an odd noise made her stop for a moment. She ventured into the yard. At first she wondered if the world had finally gone mad, for her neighbors were spilling out of their homes into the street. They were dancing and shouting in obvious celebration. It made no sense to her until she looked to where many of them were pointing. On the summit of Mount Namsan flew a South Korean flag alongside a United Nations flag.

She later learned that General MacArthur had led a risky amphibious landing at Incheon. His strategy included 75,000 troops and 261 naval vessels. Part of the plan involved making the North Korean People's Army (NKPA) believe the Americans would land at Kunsan, which is farther south than Incheon. The South Korean army, now reinvigorated by the Americans, pushed its way north from Busan, the southern port city. This surprise attack and decisive victory had forced the NKPA to retreat. MacArthur and his troops recaptured Seoul and cut several important NKPA supply lines. Though many believed General MacArthur's plan risky, it turned out to be a history-making and brilliantly executed operation.

The welcome arrival of the American soldiers brought relief in the form of hope and food. The troops generously distributed army ration boxes to the hungry residents.

Mom's command of the English language afforded her an advantage over other Koreans. She instantly became the neighborhood translator, bridging the communication barrier between Korean citizens and American troops.

Grateful for her help, the American soldiers befriended my mother. In exchange for her aid, they located her mother, who was living in Daejeon, a large city in central Korea, about ninety miles south of Seoul.

So with me bound to her back and her meager belongings in tow, my mother said good-bye to her neighbors and moved south to Daejeon. When we arrived, she took what money she had and bought a small home.

My mother was still young, in her twenties. She wanted to get married, and she needed to make a living. But her chances of accomplishing either were next to impossible with an obviously half-American child. So she went back to Seoul, where her prospects were better, and left me in the care of my grandmother.

Chapter Three

CHILDHOOD

OF COURSE, I HAD NO RECOLLECTION of all that had happened to Mother and me in Seoul. All I know is what she told me. But I have several memories of living with Grandma and my many cousins.

Grandma's life was hard. She'd lived through two world wars and the Japanese occupation. She lost her husband and then endured the Korean War. She suffered many other tragedies in her life as well, but she was strong. She had the will to press on, and she emerged from every tragedy as a survivor, never a victim.

In addition to taking me in, Grandmother also cared for her daughter-in-law and six grandchildren. Grandmother's only son, the one whose name my mother registered as my father, had died from tuberculosis, a common ailment back then.

Mom faithfully sent money every month to cover

the costs of raising me. I'm not sure how she did it, but Grandmother stretched those funds to feed all of us. I was content to grow up with so many kids in the house. Being the youngest had its advantages, and all my cousins loved me.

All nine of us slept in one room, and Grandma rented out the other two rooms in the house. We were poor, but we never missed a meal. Granted, they were simple meals of rice or barley with kimchee or just soy sauce. We each had only one set of clothing, but we never complained or felt shame, because most of our neighbors shared the same fate. Some didn't have enough food and went to bed hungry. That was life in post-war Korea. The only shame would have been in complaining.

I was a happy child until the day the town bullies let me know that I was different from the other kids. My light-brown hair might as well have been a neon sign advertising my American heritage. To try to hide this, Grandma took me to the barber and ordered him to shave my head. No kid had his head shaved in those days. So with hair or without hair, I was different. I resented what I considered an insult and resisted violently each time Grandmother took me to the barber shop. You'd think I would've figured out that no amount of bad behavior would change the outcome. She always won, and I always received a whipping for fighting her.

Not only was my light hair a banner announcing my American heredity, but also the fine blond hair on my arms and legs marked me as different. In the sunlight my body hair fairly sparkled. And then taunts like "Let's dig up some gold" would ensue.

From both adults and kids, I received one of two responses to my mixed lineage. Some were curious that a foreigner—which is what I looked like to them—knew the language and lived in their neighborhood (foreigners were rarely seen in those days). Others displayed their displeasure and called me names like Yankee, Big Nose, Mutt, and Undesirable, and shooed me away. We were taught in school that the Korean line had been preserved for over 5000 years and was the best in the world—a pure race. Many resented me for polluting that purity.

They teased and bullied me in school; therefore, I hated going to school. I would have been better off if I'd been one of those "invisible" kids no one pays any attention to. But I was all too visible. You couldn't help but notice the light kid among a sea of dark classmates. Even my aunt didn't want me to visit her for fear of what others might think of her.

One day a neighborhood kid found a used condom. It had probably been discarded by an American GI in the red-light zone, which was adjacent to where we were living. In front of what few friends I had, he dangled the condom in my face and claimed that it belonged to my dad. Then he made hand gestures indicating how humongous my father's penis was. From that point on, I had nightmares that mine would also become ridiculously large. It's amazing how one cruel, albeit ignorant, statement can instill fear into a child.

With every new taunt and every insult flung at me, I grew pessimistic about my future. Each word added to my growing sense of being unwanted and unloved.

When I was seven years old, a college-aged man walked along the street where I was playing with the neighborhood kids. He stopped and invited us to his church. "Follow me and I'll give you each a new pencil."

A bunch of us did exactly that, and when we arrived, he told us stories from the Bible. This was all new to me. I'd never heard such tales. I particularly liked the miracle stories of Jesus. I began attending the Sunday school, despite Grandma's strong opposition. She feared Christianity and became irate when she learned that I was giving all my allowance to the church.

I loved attending church, and it became even more exciting as Christmas approached. My mom had sent a pair of American-made, fur-lined boots to keep my feet warm in the cold Korean winters. I wore them for special occasions, like on Sundays, and I basked in the approval by those who noticed how unique they were.

One Sunday the young man who had first led

us to the church said, "We're going to practice for a play as part of the Christmas program. The play will show many different nationalities coming together to celebrate the birth of our Lord."

I'm not sure I caught the gist of what he was saying. I was more interested in learning what my role would be. My excitement grew as he assigned the different roles to the kids. When it was my turn, I fairly shook with expectancy.

"Robert, I want you to dress up as a Yankee, since you look American."

I couldn't believe my ears. The other kids broke out in raucous laughter. This guy wanted to shine a spotlight on the one thing in my life that attracted all manner of insult.

I longed for the floor to open up and swallow me whole. I ran to the back of the sanctuary. Slurs and more laughter chased me. Tears blurred my vision so that I barely found my way to the door. I stopped to put on my shoes. It was common practice to remove shoes before entering a building. But my special American-made boots were gone! Someone had stolen them. I had no choice but to walk home in the cold, barefooted and crying. When I arrived home in this condition, my grandmother made me tell her what happened.

Grandmother was a sweet lady, but she had been taught to believe that Christianity was the Western

Devil. So she had no sympathy for me. She didn't like my going to church and had warned me not to go. Therefore, my refusal to listen to her, combined with coming home without my boots, had pushed her to the limit of her patience. She was so angry that she gave me a good whipping. I cried several times that day.

This experience at the church caused me great pain. I had borne much insult and endured rejection and snubs to this point, and now to be paraded before an audience of my peers and their parents for my American looks was too much. I couldn't do it. But the most unfortunate result of this incident was my reaction to attending church. That was the last time I set foot in the church until I was twenty-five years old.

Did the young man understand my plight, and was his role assignment another form of abuse? Or was he unaware that my light hair and eyes made me a target of abuse? Had I been assigned a different role, would I have remained in church? And if so, would my life have been different? Of course, I have no answers to those questions, and it doesn't matter. For one thing, I can't go back and change one iota of the past. Most of all, God promised to use all things for my good. I believe that no experience, good or bad, is wasted when we are in God.

Looking back, I believe the young man meant no harm. I still have fond memories of him. He was committed to the Lord and loved the children so much that he always walked around the neighborhood and invited them to church. I don't think he realized his mistake.

God has used this incident to make me more understanding of people's inevitable mistakes and more forgiving of those who hurt me. The abuse I suffered while growing up in Korea has been a tool in God's hands, allowing me to identify with and counsel those who struggle with hurts and unforgiveness, assuring them that God is willing to bring good out of their bad situations.

Chapter Four

———◆———

BULLYING AND ABUSE

IT MAY SEEM ODD, BUT EVEN THOSE I considered friends called me names and bullied me to one degree or another. If I didn't play with these boys who insulted me, I would've had no one to play with at all. I had a choice: tormentor-friends or no friends. Naturally, some of the kids in school were not my friends; they were simply tormentors and treated me worse than my "friends."

One time while I was on my way home, some kids were shouting the usual insults at me. I tried to ignore them and kept walking when I felt something slam into the back of my head. I stumbled forward at the strength of the impact and instinctively put my hand on my head where I felt intense pain. Feeling warm wetness, I pulled my hand away. It was covered in blood. Then I realized that my shirt was becoming soaked in blood. Whether from the blow to my head or the sight of so much blood—or a combination of both—I grew dizzy and almost fell down. But the rocks kept coming. I had to run to avoid getting struck by more. Even as I bolted toward home, the hurled stones smacked against my back and buttocks, but I kept running until I reached home. To this day I'm not sure how I managed to make it all the way without passing out.

When I stumbled into the house with my head and shirt bloodied, Grandma let out a cry of anguish. She ordered one of my older cousins to rush me to the doctor. He hoisted me on his back, piggyback style, and carried me to the country doctor. The doctor looked at the cut while the blood was still gushing and said that he was not equipped to handle my case. He sent us to the provincial hospital, about twenty blocks away. My cousin lifted me onto his back again and sprinted like a marathon runner. By the time we arrived at the hospital, both my cousin and I were drenched in my blood. The emergency doctor later said that because I had lost so much blood, I could have died had we arrived a minute later.

While this is an extreme result of the verbal and physical abuse others pelted me with, I share it because incidents like this portray not only the culture in which I grew up but also reveal a bit about how I viewed myself. Needless to say, I was not a confident kid. Everyone treated me as though it was my fault that I was half-American and half-Korean. They accused me of dirtying Korean purity; therefore, I deserved punishment. The name calling, being singled out and shunned because of how I looked . . . all of it affected me deep inside. I couldn't talk about my feelings, because it would not have changed anything. The worst part was when I began to believe what they said was true.

Though I loved my grandmother and cousins, I missed my mom terribly. During the thirty days of summer vacation, I visited Mom in Seoul. On my first visit, I was surprised to find her married to a man I called "General," because he was not only bossy but expected his home to be in order and things done his way.

I didn't like General, but I kept my feelings to myself, and I showed him the honor expected of me. Overriding my dislike of him was my desire to be with Mom. I hated counting down that month. The days passed far too quickly, and after what seemed only a few days, it was time for me to return to Daejeon.

I begged her to let me live with her. Finally, one day she agreed, but only when I was to enter middle school—seventh grade. I jumped up and down, excited to be reunited with my mother after all this time. But then she added a condition. "Only if you pass the entrance exam to get into one of the top elite schools."

Her stipulation knocked my feet from under me. What she asked was unfeasible, like the proverbial leopard changing its spots.

My mother knew it was impossible for a country boy from a country elementary school to beat out the brighter city kids and pass the stringent entrance exam. The odds were stacked against me. She loved me and wanted me near her, but she knew that having me live with her and my stepfather would put a strain on their relationship. Besides that, my American blood would cause additional tension with Mother's in-laws. I figured she'd made this requirement because she assumed I couldn't meet it.

In those days, all Korean students had to take three major examinations that usually governed their future career paths. The intensity of the competition put horrendous stress on young children. The first of the three exams was taken in sixth grade. How the child ranked in this first-level testing determined which middle school he or she could attend. The higher the score, the better-ranking school he or she got into. And, of course, the level of school the child attended affected future prospects.

Let's say that from a young age you always wanted to be a doctor. Toward the end of sixth grade, you took an exam that would decide which school you would attend for the next few years. Of course, to be a doctor, you need to get into the top-ranking schools. You take the exam at the school you desire to attend. The higher ranking the school, the tougher the exam. If your score isn't high enough, you cannot attend this school, which, in turn, jeopardizes your chance of qualifying for the high school and college you'll need to attend to obtain a medical degree. So how you perform as an eleven-year-old affects your entire life. Very stressful, to say the least.

In addition, city schools offered an academic advantage over country schools. So for me to attend a country school and hope to get into not just a city middle school but an *elite* city school—well, it was a lofty dream at best. More like yearning for a miracle.

But I took my mother's words as a promise and a challenge. I had one school year to prepare for the entrance exam.

A few days before the beginning of sixth grade, I had nightmares of being assigned to the teacher we'd nicknamed Tiger. Every kid was scared to death of him because of the heavy workload he piled on his students. Plus he was an imposing and intimidating figure—tall, athletic, and mean.

The first day of school arrived. My nightmare became my reality. As I checked the class rosters, I found my name listed as one of Tiger's students.

Off I trudged to my classroom. Right away the

teacher set ground rules while my classmates and I sat trembling in our seats. He determined for each of us a "Must Score," a certain exam score we'd have to reach, depending on which middle school we wanted to apply for. Most of my classmates had no intention of moving, so they hoped to get into the local schools. He set their Must Score on each practice exam between 80 and 90. When I told him I wished to attend Yong San Middle School in Seoul, his eyes widened then quickly narrowed. I trembled harder.

"Robert, of all the students I've taught in my career, none who applied for that kind of school ever passed the exam." He paused and studied me for a moment. "Your Must Score is ninety-five."

A Must Score of 95 is the equivalent of straight-A work on *everything*.

If that wasn't bad enough, he announced more dreadful news. "Each day I will give you one test, maybe more." He rocked on the balls of his feet, his hands tucked behind him. "Each test will be graded. The score you receive will be subtracted from your Must Score to calculate the number of whippings I will give you."

He reached into his desk and pulled out a leather belt and a long white root from an acacia tree. Then with a loud *thwack*, he demonstrated on his desk how hard he would strike us.

I was so frightened, I wet my pants.

From that day on, I studied hard and long, sleeping only a few hours each night. Some mornings, Tiger examined our eyes to determine if we'd forsaken sleep and studied late into the night. On cold winter mornings, we opened the windows and held our eyes open, letting the icy wind dry out our eyes so they would appear bloodshot—proof of our late-night studying.

The whippings became not only a daily routine, but they also increased in severity as the tests became more difficult. The open wounds on the backs of my legs never healed between beatings.

But my dream of living with Mom in Seoul, firmly planted in my heart and mind, drove me to persevere with my studies and do everything necessary to reach my goal. Studying was one thing I could control in my life. I couldn't stop others from making fun of me. I couldn't make the bullying go away. I couldn't make myself full Korean. But I could study. I could stay up late every night and prepare for the next day's test. This part of me was totally mine to command.

Finally the day arrived that would determine my fate. I was required to take the exam at the school I hoped to get into, so I went to Seoul and entered the testing room. My country-boy appearance stood out in the midst of all those well-dressed city kids. They wore sharp-looking sweaters or winter coats, and their hair was neatly combed. I wore my ratty, patched school uniform, and Grandma had won another round at the barber's, so my head was closely shaved.

But the biggest difference I saw was that those city kids looked smarter than me, and every kid wore a watch—except me! Back then, wearing a watch was a status symbol. I had several strikes against me that day: clothing, hair (or lack thereof), no watch, country education, and a big dose of fear. To say I felt intimidated and nervous doesn't come close to my experience. It was so bad that, to this day, I don't remember how I got through the exam.

Now the waiting began. It would be days before I learned the results of an examination that reflected the culmination of almost a year of concentrated work. Remember, I was only twelve years old when I began pursuing this near-impossible goal. I had endured months of intense study, daily beatings, and little sleep. Yet the five days of waiting for the score were the most agonizing and horrific. I stopped eating and became so malnourished, my gums turned black. I was literally worrying myself to death. Mom became concerned because I couldn't swallow. She tried spoon-feeding me sweet syrup, hoping some nourishment would trickle down my throat.

The one thing I wanted was to be with my mother in the modern environment of Seoul. I was keenly aware of what failure would mean. I'd have to return to Daejeon. As much as I loved my grandmother and cousins, going back would devastate me.

Finally, late one evening, the word came that the test results were being posted on the school's fence. Filled with both anxiety and anticipation, Mom and I hurried to the school. When we arrived, a crowd had already gathered. Several pages comprised the list. The names of those who had been accepted were handwritten with a broad brush in Chinese calligraphy, the form of writing used by the elite.

The names were not in alphabetical order, so we had to read every name on each sheet of paper until we found the one we were hoping to see—mine—or came to the end. The lighting was poor, so reading the list was difficult. Some people thought to bring flashlights, which helped a bit. As those around us hunted for the one name that meant so much to them, a cacophony of yells, sobs, and shouts filled the night air.

Then Mom screamed.

I stopped breathing. I had failed. No doubt she believed my failure would send me over the edge.

She grabbed me by my arms and shook me to get my attention. I feared seeing the disappointment in her eyes. But I did look up. She was jabbering something. I struggled to make out her words.

"Robert, did you hear me?" She shook me again.

"You passed! You passed the exam, Robert!" She pulled me into a tight embrace.

Surely she was mistaken. I struggled out of her arms. I had to see my name for myself. I pushed through the crowd and squeezed to the front. I started reading from the beginning. I stopped when I read my Korean name—Chulsoo Park. It was true. I had passed!

I turned and shoved through the screaming, crying mass, searching frantically for Mom. I spotted her dancing in the street with others who shared in the celebration. Buses and cars—all traffic—had come to a halt.

The relief that surged through me was like a gust of sweet, fresh air. In fact, I felt like I could start breathing again. I wanted to dance with joy with my mother, but all of a sudden weariness sapped my last bit of strength. Knowing I'd reached my goal, my senses were awakening so that I felt intense hunger and exhaustion at the same time.

I would stay in Seoul and not return to Daejeon. So began the next chapter of my life.

But all was not rosy.

My stepfather remained distant. He didn't say a word about my accomplishment; neither did he welcome me into their home. In fact, he never spoke to me, never acknowledged my existence. Whenever he received his paycheck, he left the house and didn't come home for days. He stayed out, gambling away most of the income. On days he didn't gamble, he went fishing. That suited me just fine, because when he was home, the atmosphere his presence created set me on edge. And I wasn't the only one who suffered.

In those days we had live-in housemaids, not because we were wealthy, but because the labor was so cheap. We provided them with a room to sleep in, food to eat, and a meager salary. Most of these maids came from the countryside and were usually in their teens. My stepfather sexually abused these girls and impregnated several of them. Each time Mom would be forced into the position of paying for the damages, including the cost of an abortion.

Mom couldn't hide her agony. I saw it in the worry lines of her brow. I saw it in her downcast eyes. I saw it in every forced smile.

I assumed guilt for the mounting strain between my mother and stepfather. In retrospect, I came to understand that I was not the cause of the deterioration of their relationship, for they had been experiencing trouble before I moved in. But at the time, I believed I was the cause, which added to my inferior feelings.

Though I had left behind my life in the country, some things followed me. The name calling, the taunts, the bullying clung to me like a tick on a deer. Accusations of polluting the Korean lineage haunted me. Though I was half-Korean, most nationals wouldn't accept me as Korean. I became pessimistic about my future, doubting that I would ever marry, because no Korean family would allow a daughter to be the wife of a man of mixed blood. Worry became my companion as I struggled to find my place in the country of my birth.

In my new school, I was under intense pressure not only to keep up with my studies but to excel in them. But I began to ask myself why I should work so hard. If my future looked so bleak, why torture myself with trying to be the best in my class? My self-image was so low and my inferiority complex so strong that I did what made sense to me at the time. I hung out with friends who were in a similar situation—all were raised without their fathers. We were a band of brothers who had simply given up on life. We did all the things we weren't supposed to do: smoke, womanize, drink, and fight, all the while listening to Elvis and The Beatles. We simply killed time and neglected our studies.

Around that same time, Mom became pregnant with my sister. She hoped that a baby would force General to take an interest in her and the family. When my half sister, Yuni, was born, he was almost beside himself with adoration for his daughter. As my mother had hoped, General transformed into a family man.

I also fell in love with Yuni. She was the greatest and perhaps only joy in my life at the time.

Chapter Five

———◆———

PEARL S. BUCK

PEARL S. BUCK, THE FAMED AUTHOR, SPENT most of her young life in China. Her writing of Chinese life came from her firsthand knowledge and understanding of the culture. Her books served to enlighten Westerners to that way of life.

When Pearl learned that adoption services in the United States considered Asian and mixed-race children unadoptable, she founded Welcome House in 1949, the first international, interracial adoption agency. Then in 1965, at age seventy-three, she started the Pearl S. Buck Foundation to support children thought to be ineligible for adoption.

In that same year, she hoped to go back to China, but the Communists refused her request; therefore, she visited Korea. She had been studying the history and culture of Korea and had chosen this country as the setting for her next book. One of the first places she visited was an orphanage. By then she'd adopted several girls, including an African German, two Japanese, and an American, who were all living in Philadelphia.

As she studied the children in the Seoul orphanage, she noticed that several of the children had light-colored hair and eyes—some even had blue eyes. Having grown up in China, she knew these children could not be fully Asian.

"Where did these children come from?" she asked the orphanage director through her interpreter, Ms. Lee.

"They are abandoned children, fathered by American GIs."

"How many of these Amerasians [a term she coined] are in Korea?"

Pearl was shocked when Ms. Lee translated the answer from the orphanage director. "Fifty thousand in Korea and at least that many in Vietnam, Japan, and the Philippines."

Whether or not the US government was aware of the problem, it was obvious to Ms. Buck that no one was addressing the issue.

Then she began to ask more questions. "Are there any Amerasian children other than the ones living in orphanages? If so, how are their lives different? Are any successfully living in homes and attending school rather than abandoned to live in orphanages?"

No one had any answers, so she asked Ms. Lee, who

was also a social worker, to find any children that fit this description.

Ms. Lee sent out three assistants to canvass Seoul, a city of ten million people. How Ms. Lee had heard about an Amerasian youth attending a prestigious high school was nothing short of miraculous.

I was in biology class when the principal's secretary interrupted the teacher, called me out of the room, and escorted me to the school office. Of course, I was scared. But I couldn't think of anything I had done that would merit a visit to the principal. The secretary guided me into the office. Sitting in the principal's chair was not the principal, but a woman I didn't recognize. She got right down to business.

"I am Ms. Lee. I am Pearl S. Buck's interpreter. Do you know who Ms. Buck is?"

"Yes, of course. The famous writer. I heard she was visiting Korea." I was glad not to be in any trouble, but I was befuddled by Ms. Lee's presence and her question.

"Ms. Buck would like to interview you for her next book."

Pearl S. Buck wanted to interview me? That was like James Patterson asking to interview you for his next book. Stunned, I'm not sure what I said, but I agreed.

On the designated day, Mom and I sat across from Ms. Buck and Theodore (Ted) Harris, her companion and later the CEO of the Pearl S. Buck Foundation. My first impression of her was not exactly what I expected. I had figured her to be enthusiastic to interview me. I pictured her full of compassion and love. But she was none of those things. In fact, she seemed just the opposite: impersonal and aloof.

After asking a few questions, she instructed Harris to continue the interview. She sat next to him as he questioned me about my life. He was far more engaging and compassionate.

And then she abruptly stood. "I am fatigued. We shall terminate the interview."

Speechless, I arose from my chair. But my mother remained seated, as though refusing to be dismissed. Then she embarrassed me by breaking down, crying and pleading with Ms. Buck.

"You have no idea what these mixed-bloods are going through in Korea. You are not even asking the right questions because you don't care—you Americans don't care about taking any responsibility for your offspring. These are your people. My son is not Korean; he is American because the Korean society views him as such. He is an excellent student and yet has no future in this country. Do you think he will get a job? Do you think anyone will give him their daughter in marriage? He carries the symbol of dishonor on his face. Is that his fault he was born that way? He is a good kid, and I am proud of him, but it breaks my heart to read in his diary his thoughts of suicide. Please, take my son to the United States. He is smart and will do well there. He will never disappoint you. He has no life here." She cradled her face in her hands and sobbed.

I was angry that she had not only read my diary but also told Pearl Buck and Ted Harris about it. I was mortified at her emotional display. I wanted to get out of there without delay.

But Ms. Buck seemed immediately energized. Her eyes were bright with interest as she addressed me. "You keep a diary? How long have you been doing that? Is it possible for me to read it?"

I opened my mouth to say no.

Mom jumped up. "Of course!"

Ms. Buck turned to Ms. Lee. "Go with Robert and his mother and pick up the diary. Translate it."

Ms. Lee gathered her belongings. "I will drive them to their home and get the diary, but it may take some time to translate it."

"I don't care if it takes all night. Bring the translation to breakfast tomorrow. We're leaving soon, and I want to take the diary with me."

She spoke of my diary, which held my personal thoughts and experiences, as though she owned it. Things were happening so fast. I had no say in the matter.

Forty years later, an obscure Korean publisher

approached me and said that they were translating a book by Pearl S. Buck titled *New Year* and asked me to write the introduction. I agreed to do so, and as I was reading it, I could not believe my eyes. Although she had inserted some fictional parts, Pearl S. Buck had based her novel on my story. She had never told me about the book, let alone asked for my permission.

It would seem she accomplished both of her purposes for visiting Korea. She and Harris had found a "successful" Amerasian child and the seeds for her next book—a translated version of my diary. But they didn't respond to my mother's plea to take me to America. However, the Foundation, which had an office in Seoul, did award me a scholarship.

In early June 1967, two years after my "interview," the newspapers reported that Buck was visiting Korea to establish the first overseas office for the Pearl S. Buck Foundation. I had just been accepted at the prestigious Yonsei University in Seoul. Founded in 1915 by Methodist missionary Horace Grant Underwood, Yonsei is the equivalent to America's Ivy League schools. Upon entering the school, my life took a turn for the better. I left behind the stress of the application process and examinations of getting into college. I stepped into an adult world, abandoned teenage angst, and enjoyed the freedom to do what I wanted. But most of all, I was more accepted by others. My new clothes and stylish haircut helped me to become popular among the female students. Even my stepfather, though still not speaking to me, appeared to have second thoughts about me.

I did not think too much of Buck's visit when I read about it, so I was surprised when a messenger came to me with a request that I visit the author at her hotel. When I arrived in her suite, she and Harris welcomed me as though they'd found a lost son.

Harris embraced me and then dropped the bomb. "Robert, we are taking you with us to the United States. There you can pursue your dream of becoming a doctor."

I'm not sure how long I stood there with my mouth hanging open. I wondered if this was for real, or just a set-up for another big disappointment.

I finally found my voice. "I would like to go to America, but I cannot."

Harris and Buck exchanged questioning looks.

"All males under the age of thirty are required to complete three years of military duty. There are no exceptions. I cannot leave the country without first fulfilling this requirement."

Serving in the military had always been a huge fear of mine. The Korean army was known to use violence and an inhumane level of training, including frequent beatings and punishments. Because of my mixed race, I would receive a double portion of that kind of treatment. I wasn't sure I could survive it.

"Miss Buck, if you would please keep your promise of taking me to the United States in three years, I will join the army today to fulfill President Park's demand."

She studied me for a moment. "Well, tomorrow I have an invitation to visit the president at the Blue House. I will see what I can do about that."

I shook my head. "He will not issue an exception. You don't understand Korea. You don't understand President Park; we Koreans fear him. Please, don't mention my name. If you do, I can be in all kinds of trouble."

But God, not Ms. Buck, not even the president of Korea, was in control of my life. Unbeknownst to us all, God had already set up His plan. A French film crew was following Buck, making a documentary on her life and work. They filmed every move she made and took a special interest in my case. When she visited the Foreign Ministry with me in tow, the entire French crew, with their extended microphones and lighting and cameras, followed. Everywhere we went, we drew so much attention I felt like a movie star.

To my utter astonishment, the Korean government not only made an exception for my draft but also issued a passport within a day—all fees waived. The consul at the US Embassy granted my visa on the spot, and all of a sudden I was free to leave the country. Of course, no one considered that this miracle was from the hand of God. Not even I knew that. But looking back, it is the only explanation.

I said good-bye to my mother and family. Pearl S. Buck, Theodore Harris, Buck's staff, and I left Korea on June 15, 1967. I was eighteen years old.

Chapter Six

———◆———

DREAM IN ENGLISH

PEARL S. BUCK CALLED ME TO THE FIRST-class section of the plane, where she and Harris were seated.

"Robert, you must learn the English language as quickly as you can so you'll have no problem with your studies and your life in America in general. I want you to speak English only—no Korean at all. Do you understand?"

What right did she have to take away my mother tongue? But I had no choice in the matter. My life was in her hands. "How long do I need to speak only English? Forever?"

"When you begin to dream in English, that's a sure sign you have achieved mastery in the language. So no speaking Korean until you dream in English."

That was a tall order. Anyone who speaks secondary languages knows that it takes a while to understand

and think in a language other than the native tongue. Expressing feelings and convictions in a secondary language is the hardest. Dreaming in a second language is totally out of a person's conscious control.

I wondered if I would ever dream in English and, if so, how long it would take.

Before flying on to Hawaii, we spent a few days in Tokyo, where we picked up two Amerasians, Paul and Karl, whose fathers were also American GIs. Paul reminded me of Omar Sharif. He was a few years older than I and grew up in an orphanage. He had attended the prestigious Tokyo University.

Karl was two years my junior and was raised in Kyoto by his Japanese mother and stepfather.

On our first day in Honolulu, Ted Harris took Paul, Karl, and me to a department store. There he bought us each a full wardrobe. None of us was accustomed to having so many changes of clothing. We ate in first-class restaurants and toured the beautiful island of Oahu. Harris spent lavishly, and we were all grateful.

After about a week, we flew to Los Angeles and then took a car to Laguna Beach. So many new things impressed me. I craned my neck to see the tall palm trees. It seemed everyone drove big, shiny cars. Automobiles in Korea were small and packed full. To my thinking, the big, flashy cars in America could hold twenty people, yet only one or two people usually occupied them.

Surfers were an exciting oddity to me. Typically they had long hair (the long-hair phase of the '60s had not hit Korea) and carried funny-shaped boards in their cars and on the beach. But to see them ride the rolling and crashing waves was an extraordinary first-time sight.

Everywhere I looked I saw evidence of affluence: numerous department stores filled with every possible item a person could need or want, several grocery stores bulging with food. Mansions lined the coastal highway, each one displaying lavish landscaping, flaunting walls of windows, showing off tennis courts and swimming pools—the apparent wealth was everywhere.

We were in America, the land of prosperity.

I had finally made it to my fatherland. My Korean countrymen refused to see me as a Korean, so I would find my place here as an American. America was where I belonged.

But most people I met did not think I was American. Though my skin seemed fair to Koreans, to Americans it seemed dark. I was mistaken for Japanese or South American, or even Hawaiian. All I had to do was open my mouth and speak to confirm that I was not an American, for my accent gave me away as a foreigner. Any mention that my father was American seemed to make no difference. I stopped bringing him up after a while.

In Korea, I was deemed an American; in America, I was considered a foreigner. This puzzled and confused me. Who the heck was I?

We left LA in July 1967 and flew to Philadelphia. Harris took Paul, and Karl, and me to the headquarters of the Pearl S. Buck Foundation on Delancey Place. This would be our residence as well.

Pearl lived on her 300-acre property in Perkasie, Bucks County, complete with a tennis court, swimming pools, barns, a greenhouse, and several guest houses. But she also kept a bedroom suite on the third floor of the Foundation building.

When she stayed at the Foundation, Harris would always accompany her to her suite after dinner and take a long time to say goodnight. He'd hug her and kiss her on the cheeks. We boys used to hide behind the fifth floor railing and watch. We thought it odd and concluded it was more than an American custom, but we couldn't figure out a reasonable explanation.

Another observation led me to believe Harris and Pearl's relationship went beyond the employer-employee relationship. Whenever Harris accompanied Ms. Buck, he offered her his arm, certainly a gentlemanly thing to do, especially considering her advanced age of seventy-five. But she looked at him as no employee; rather, more like a woman very fond of her companion. She addressed Harris as "my dear" or "my love." It seemed strange because Harris was almost forty years younger than Ms. Buck, but again I decided it must be the American way.

Harris had another constant companion: Jimmy Pauls, a fat, greasy type who ate like a slob, drove like a maniac, and had a bad temper. These men shared the same bedroom. We would often hear them shouting and arguing—about what, we never discovered.

Paul, Karl, and I began ESL (English as Second Language) courses at the University of Pennsylvania. I had learned English while in school in Korea, but I had to improve my skills, along with reaching the goal of dreaming in English. I worked hard to develop my English and to think in the language, as Pearl had demanded.

About three months later, I finally did it. I dreamed in English! It was a "Wow!" moment. It gave me a huge sense of accomplishment. The next morning I ran to Pearl, who sat at the breakfast table. "I dreamed in English!"

She spread marmalade on her toast and set down her knife as she bit into the bread. She slowly enjoyed the bite and then patted her mouth with her napkin. "Now you can speak Korean."

I was thrilled to be "released" to speak Korean once again. But there weren't many Koreans in Philly back then, and I had no reason to seek them out, so I stuck to speaking English.

After one semester of ESL, Harris and Pearl believed I was ready to enroll in college. In Korea, I had attended Yonsei University for only three months (school there begins in March). It was likely that I would have to begin college all over.

Harris and Pearl took me to Princeton University to meet with the chancellor. Convinced I was a genius (I assure you, I am not), Harris insisted that I should be accepted with no requirements.

The chancellor seemed honored to have Pearl S. Buck visit him but escorted us to the admissions director. He questioned me about my previous schooling and determined that I would be better prepared for American college if I repeated the twelfth grade at a prep school. He also assured us he would guarantee my admission to Princeton upon successful completion of twelfth grade. No doubt the school desired to add Ms. Buck's name to their donor list.

I enrolled in Friends Select High School, a Quaker private school located in downtown Philly. Going back to high school was a culture shock, and it somewhat restricted my freedom. Most of the kids were from well-to-do families, smart, and mature for their age.

The studies challenged me. Most of the courses required reading several books a week. Back in Korea, we hardly read outside our textbooks. But here I had to read *The Iliad* and *The Odyssey* for English class.

During the second week of school, I was to take a test on *The Iliad.* As I did back home, I memorized the entire content of the epic poem by staying up all night. I felt confident I would do well on relaying any facts or reciting any part of the work. The next day the teacher handed out the tests. Eager to get started, I turned over the test paper and froze. Two essay questions comprised the test: 1) State your thoughts on the poem; and 2) State why you liked or disliked it.

This type of test is normal for the American classroom, but to the Korean student, it's unheard of. In Korea, we were taught to memorize the material so we could regurgitate any fact or detail. But to analyze its merits or formulate an opinion on it was a foreign concept. I was at a loss, so I wrote what I knew: detailed information of the poem. The teacher was not impressed and wanted to see me after the following class. She gave me an F and told me that I had not done what she had asked.

I realized then how different American education was from what I was used to. It took me a long time to realign myself. Although I did poorly for a while in English, history, and social studies, I excelled in math and physics. In fact, I impressed the class and the instructor by correcting his mistakes in teaching calculus. The irony was that in Korea, I received below-average grades in math and excelled in all other subjects.

But one of my most intriguing experiences at Friends Select was the chapel hour every morning. Unlike most religious schools, whose chapel services are presided over by a leader and typically include a song or two, prayer, and a short message, the teachers and students at this Quaker school sat quietly in the auditorium for the entire hour. Once in a while, someone would stand and talk about some revelation he'd had. That someone was always one of the teachers. I normally used that hour to catch some sleep.

We also had a devotional before we began classes. Students took turns reading from the Scripture or any religious or meditative material. I considered myself a Buddhist, although I knew virtually nothing about Buddhism.

I asked Ms. Buck for a good Buddhist passage to read to the class when my turn came. She had thousands of books in her library and pulled one out for me. She was knowledgeable about Buddhism and explained what the passage meant. Looking back, I find it interesting that she never took the opportunity to introduce Christian beliefs to me. In fact, I found no evidence that she was a practicing Christian, though she was born to missionary parents. In the three years I lived with her, I never saw her pray, go to church, or read the Bible, let alone talk about the gospel.

Chapter Seven

———◆———

CREATED CRISES

A FTER ONLY TWO MONTHS IN FRIENDS Select, I was pulled out of class. Ted Harris had sent an urgent message to the school, instructing me to return to the Foundation headquarters. At first I thought something had happened to Mom.

When I returned to the headquarters, Harris was agitated. "There is a revolt in our Korean office. The staff is attempting to take over our property in Sosa. Ms. Buck and I are flying to Seoul on the next plane, but we will have to hide you somewhere in LA while we're gone."

"Hide me? Why?"

Harris stopped pacing and studied me for a moment. "Sit down, Robert."

I obeyed.

He sat next to me and cleared his throat. "While in Korea, Ms. Buck saw an opportunity to buy seventy-five acres of land on which several buildings stand. She wants to create an orphanage for Amerasian children. But current Korean law bars foreigners from acquiring real estate. So the only way to purchase this property from a major pharmaceutical company was . . . uh, to use your name, since you are a Korean citizen."

The more I listened, the more upset I became.

"Now, Robert, I know we should have said something to you, but we were certain you'd be in favor of the project. The Foundation is a mighty good work, and, well, you can see that this orphanage will be a great help to other Amerasian children in Korea." He patted me on the back.

It took me a moment to gather my tumbling thoughts. I had many questions. In Korea, real estate transactions are finalized with a person's seal rather than signature. The seal is a stamp with the person's name.

"How were you able to use my name to buy property? I did not use my seal; in fact, I don't have a seal."

Harris drummed his fingers. "Well, now, that really isn't any concern right now. The fact is that we must deal with the situation to protect the Foundation . . . and you, my boy."

"I don't understand why I must be protected. I didn't do anything."

"The property is worth a great deal. I fear someone

might kidnap you for ransom or to force you to sign over the property. So until Ms. Buck and I return, I'm sending you to stay with people I trust."

I still had no idea what all this meant. It sounded like a scene out of a movie. I was upset that Pearl and Harris might have illegally created a seal and used my name to make an unlawful real estate purchase. In essence, I had no choice but to go along with their plan.

They took me to stay with a Greek family in LA. These were relatives of Jimmy Pauls, whom I later learned was Harris's boyfriend.

A week later, Harris and Pearl returned. When they picked me up in LA, all they said was that everything was okay, but they wouldn't discuss it further.

I returned to school and poured myself into my studies. But after only a month, I was again pulled out of school. This time I was to go with Buck and Harris on a tour of the United States to raise funds for the Pearl S. Buck Foundation. Since we traveled by car, I missed a whole month of classes, and it concerned me how this would affect my grades and thus my ability to get into Princeton.

Pearl had speaking engagements in various cities and usually was invited to go on local TV and radio interviews. She would take Harris and me on these appearances and introduce me as the fruit of sacrificial donations the viewers made to the Foundation. We did this dog and pony show in every city. After a while, I got to be very good at it. Money flooded into the office in Philly.

Ms. Buck sometimes picked up major donors along the way, too, one of whom was Dr. Richard Wilson of Tucson, Arizona, an heir of substantial oil money. He gave so much money that Harris eventually put him on the board of directors.

Spending time with Pearl had some benefits. While on the road for so many hours and days, we had many discussions on various topics. She would teach me English vocabulary and spelling, and she gave me lessons in US history. She also possessed vast knowledge of Asian history, including that of Korea. One of our interesting exchanges was about John F. Kennedy and who had killed him. She thought Lyndon B. Johnson engineered the whole thing and said, "He is an evil man."

One thing I learned from spending so much time with Ms. Buck was her rigidly disciplined lifestyle, which I started to emulate. She arose early every morning and spent a few hours writing. That is how she was able to author almost a hundred books in her lifetime. An avid reader, she averaged a book a day. When not traveling, she played the piano regularly. She was always busy, always doing something. Even at her advanced age, she never took naps.

In comparison, Ted Harris was almost the opposite. He was an eighth-grade dropout, almost never read books, smoked constantly, and drank every day. He was from Bamberg, South Carolina. Prior to meeting Pearl, he worked as a dance instructor at an Arthur Murray Dance Studio in Jenkintown, Pennsylvania. And yet he ably engaged in intelligent conversation and articulated his thoughts succinctly. He had a good memory and, therefore, learned new information quickly and retained it. He possessed immaculate manners and at all times dressed impeccably. He was an impressive actor.

Ms. Buck didn't like Martin Luther King Jr. for "agitating the blacks." She said that the riots and burning in major cities, including Philly, after his assassination proved her point. She often agreed with Harris, who made derogatory remarks about African Americans.

I thought it odd that these two would have this racist attitude while operating a foundation designed to help mixed-race children. I was learning more about American culture, and their position on civil rights was just one of many things that baffled me.

Chapter Eight

———◆———

TROUBLING TIMES

PAUL, KARL, AND I LIVED AT THE Foundation headquarters with another kid named Sam. Sam had been residing there before we three arrived in 1967, though he had been raised in the same orphanage in Tokyo as Paul.

Sam was tall. He had a dark complexion. His prominent nose and large eyes made me wonder if he was part Jewish. He was an accomplished pianist on scholarship at the Philadelphia School of Music and had an eccentric and arrogant side to him.

Paul was the quiet, thoughtful type. He never liked to talk much about how he was adjusting to life in America or what he thought about school, people, or issues. He kept everything bottled up.

Karl was the epitome of a typical teenager, somewhat emotional and immature.

Though we lived together, learned to reside in

America, and were a band of mixed-race young men, I can't say that I either liked or disliked them. We were thrust together and made the best of it, but we never bonded.

One night, Sam, Paul, and Karl came to my room and said they wanted to talk about something. I invited them in, but they said what they needed to discuss was better done somewhere other than the Foundation building.

We went to a pub and each ordered some German beer. As we settled into a booth at the back of the bar, Paul was the first to speak up in his halting English. "When we all were still in that Hilton Hotel in Tokyo, Harris had me alone in his room. He asked me strange questions about homosexual activities in my orphanage. Even though I told him I was not aware of any such goings on, he insisted that some boys must have touched each other and had anal sex. And then he touched me and kissed me. I did not like it, but I really wanted to go to America, so I let him. I hate myself for letting him do that to me. But now what I regret the most is leaving Japan. I was well on my way to becoming a lawyer. Now I am stuck here with no future. I am nothing. He screwed up my life!" His eyes welled with tears as he spoke.

Sam jumped in. "One time I saw Harris and Pauls having sex. Have you noticed how Harris cries like a little girl when he gets drunk? I am telling you, this Foundation is infested with homosexuals. Davis [VP], Wood [Administrator], Kearney [Harris's personal secretary]: they are all gays. Harris has surrounded himself with gays. And now we have been brought into this trap! And the sad thing is that Ms. Buck doesn't have a clue."

As Paul and Sam went on, I thought about the times I'd seen Harris use the Foundation credit cards and write checks to purchase not just personal items but also luxuries: diamond rings, rubies, and several tailored suits. He'd even bought expensive cars like a Daimler, Lincoln, Jeep, a few antique automobiles, and a yacht with Foundation money. "Ms. Buck needs to know this. She has been conned, big-time."

So the four of us decided to visit her at her personal residence in Bucks County, where she was spending the weekend.

Sam didn't want to make waves and eventually copped out. So Paul, Karl, and I decided to go through with telling her what we knew. Even if it meant being sent back to our countries, we would do the right thing. So we drove to Perkasie, Bucks County, and paid an unannounced visit. Since my English was better than Paul and Karl's, I became the spokesperson. We arrived early in the evening, but her estate lay in darkness.

Nervous as turkeys before Thanksgiving, we

knocked on the door. Ms. Buck answered it herself. We nearly freaked, because she was wearing her pajamas, her long white hair flowing down her back rather than pinned up, and she had no teeth! Even at that, she invited us in, showed us to the living room, and had us sit down.

I hadn't said much about our experiences and observations of Harris before her smile faded and her eyes became hard. The more I talked, the deeper she frowned. Her displeasure conveyed that we were fighting a losing battle.

When I was finished, she didn't say a word but picked up the phone and called Harris, who was staying at the Hilltop House, which was part of Pearl Buck's immense estate.

"I have the boys here. You need to come over in a hurry. I have no idea what they are up to. I think someone's been feeding them some wrong ideas about you."

We tried not to fidget while we waited for Harris to arrive, yet we couldn't help but squirm a bit. I kept wiping away beads of sweat that popped up on my brow.

Pearl ignored Paul and Karl, but pinned me with a look. "Robert, I am terribly disappointed in you. I always thought you were brighter than the other boys. In fact, you were my favorite, as well as Mr. Harris's. You have no appreciation of what Mr. Harris has done for you. What would your mother say about this? I am so ashamed of you."

Harris used the four-wheel-drive Jeep to cut across the field rather than drive around the longer roadway. Harris arrived with a very different attitude: compassionate and understanding rather than joining Ms. Buck in condemning our actions. "These poor boys are responding out of the terrible treatment they received in their upbringings. Pearl, it's further proof that the Foundation's work is crucial in saving these children. If I must suffer false accusations for the sake of the Foundation's success, it's a price I gladly pay. You know that several people are jealous of my success here at the Foundation, so I fear they have gotten hold of these boys and are manipulating them to do their dirty work in hopes of toppling me."

Pearl studied the three of us a moment. "You're right, Ted."

Then the two of them talked to us, warning us against listening to idle gossip. They cautioned us to be watchful against being used by others who oppose the Foundation's work.

We knew what we'd seen, and we knew that speaking up was the ethical thing to do. Yet we'd been marginalized—even manipulated while at the same time being cautioned against being manipulated.

No one spoke a word all the way back to Philly.

From that day on, we three became the outcasts of the Foundation. We were moved out of our bedrooms and relocated to the loft of another building. Our only furniture was a mattress on the floor. All allowances stopped. When the cold months arrived, we had no coats to wear. Harris had told us when we left Korea and Japan that we didn't need to bring ours, because he would buy us new ones. That promise was obviously rescinded.

The weather wasn't the only cold we suffered from. The treatment we received from others at the Foundation also turned frigid. Where we once dined with Pearl and Harris in the lavishly decorated dining room on the second floor of the Foundation, we now ate in the basement kitchen. The food was barely edible. I'm not sure the rats would have eaten it. Even the housemaids turned against us. They avoided all contact with us. When we did encounter them, they were often verbally abusive to us.

It's difficult to describe that time of my life. It was as if a palpable darkness had descended over me and sucked the color from everything. I had no one to turn to. As hard as I tried, I couldn't figure a way out of my predicament.

Well, one option was to return to Korea. But every time that thought emerged, I beat it down, because my current state was actually better than what I would have in Korea. When I left my country, I left for good. All my friends and relatives understood it that way. If I returned, I would be seen as a failure. More shame would be heaped upon me. It would devastate my mother. But on top of all this, to return to my country of birth would result in immediate induction into the Korean army. That in itself was a worse nightmare than the one I lived at this time. Hopelessness and misery became my constant companions.

Then out of the blue, Harris called me to the board room in the main building. I was totally surprised to find Chuck and John, my two Amerasian buddies from Seoul. I learned that in the spring of 1968, Harris and Pearl had gone to Korea and decided to bring Chuck and John to America, along with four girls.

Chuck was a year older than I was. He was street smart and a street fighter. He wouldn't tolerate bullying or even a biased look tossed his way. It always amazed me how much alcohol he could consume.

John had grown up in an orphanage and had received very little formal education, yet he too was savvy in fighting his way to survival. He was tall and masculine, with wavy hair. When he was thirteen, a female social worker at his orphanage introduced him to sex. She was the first of several who abused him.

All his life he thought he had only one relative, an aunt. On the day of his departure from Korea to come to America, this "aunt" had showed up to say good-bye. But just before he was to board the plane, she confessed that she was his mother. She had previously told him that his mother had died shortly after giving birth to him. So to learn this truth cut him to the core. He had no time to get the answers to many questions: Why did she lie to him? Was she ashamed of him so she claimed to be his aunt and abandoned him? What little self-worth he had then plummeted. To this day, he struggles with this issue about his aunt-mother.

One of the four girls was Shirley, a dark-skinned, shapely girl who looked Hispanic. When she was about ten years old, her father had gone to Korea to find her. He came back to California with Shirley. But she didn't like her stepmother and missed her mother terribly, so she eventually returned to Korea. When I first met her at the Foundation office in Seoul, after my first interview with Harris and Buck, she came on to me, but I already had a girlfriend and wasn't interested. Yet we remained good friends.

It was like a breath of fresh air to be with old friends, yet my present circumstances hung over me like a menacing thunderhead.

What I didn't understand at the time was that this reunion was all part of Harris's strategy to manipulate me further. By isolating me, allowing the staff to mistreat me, and then bringing my friends from Korea, he intended to mend the relationship with me and also restore his reputation. He was especially targeting to get me back on his side. Whether it was because he genuinely favored me or thought I was the key in this plan, I still do not know to this day.

I was lonely and desperate, and reuniting me with friends was the bait I readily took. I decided to cooperate with Harris. I once again traveled with him and Buck as they conducted their fund-raising events. I kept Harris company on his shopping trips. And I helped the new arrivals from Korea settle in to their home at the Foundation.

Not only had Harris restored me to my former status, he also doubled my benefits by buying me a '56 classic Thunderbird and letting me drive the Jeep whenever I wanted. He gave me several credit cards, which in those days were not common and were reserved for the wealthy. I became the object of envy and popularity.

But I wasn't stupid. It didn't get past me that Paul, Karl, and Sam had not been reinstated. They all ended up leaving. Paul and Sam moved out of state to attend college. If my recall is correct, a family adopted Karl. I used caution and always kept a distance from Harris, wary that he might make unwanted advances. But truth be told, I enjoyed these benefits.

One day in the summer of '68, Harris, Pearl, and I

drove in his brand-new Lincoln Mark III to the Korean Embassy in Washington, DC, to renew my passport. On the way back, Harris decided to show me a scenic route by crossing the Chesapeake Bay Bridge and going through Delaware rather than the shorter way through Baltimore. When we arrived on the other side of the bridge, Harris and Pearl wanted to find a nice place to have dinner. We found a restaurant that had a magnificent view of the sparkling bay.

Admiring the scene as the sun glistened off the water, I casually commented, "It would be nice to have a vacation home here."

Harris jumped on that idea. "Robert is so intelligent that he continues to amaze me, don't you agree, my dear? I can see he is going to be a very successful businessman. He sees the growth potential in real estate in this area, and he is right, Pearl. There is an investment opportunity here, and we can use it for our vacations in the meantime. What a brilliant idea!"

His reaction dumbfounded me. I wasn't seriously suggesting what Harris was rambling on about. I was just sort of daydreaming. Who hasn't said a similar thing but without any intention of following through? But I kept my mouth shut and went along for the ride.

Harris asked the owner of the restaurant if any waterfront properties were for sale. As it turned out, the owner was also a real estate agent. He offered us coffee and dessert while he showed us photos of several places for sale along the shore.

Harris didn't waste any time. He had the restaurateur-Realtor take us to one of these properties. Unfortunately, we couldn't see the house well because by then darkness had settled.

Any other person would return in the daylight to see the house. But this was not Harris's way. He was impulsive and wanted what he wanted now. He made an offer, essentially sight unseen.

More amazing was that Pearl stood by, never offering a word of caution. It seemed when it came to Harris, she was passive, allowing him to do whatever he wished.

I made an inane remark about this being a nice place for a vacation home. Harris blew it way out of proportion. Pearl remained silent. It was a crazy combination.

Little did I know that this vacation property would be the place where I would be arrested some months later.

Chapter Nine

THE CANCELLATION

PRIOR TO 1965, WHEN TED HARRIS MET Pearl S. Buck, he worked as an instructor at Arthur Murray Dance Studio in Jenkintown, Pennsylvania. The studio was near the gift shop where Clarissa Brown worked. One day, Harris visited the shop and met the pleasant, intelligent, and attractive forty-four-year-old divorcee.

Though Harris eventually quit his job as dance instructor to work with Ms. Buck, he and Clarissa remained friends.

In the summer of 1968, Harris showed up in the office and introduced Clarissa as his new secretary. He was acting like a lovesick schoolboy: excited and silly. And in less than a month, he dropped a bombshell by announcing that he and Clarissa were engaged.

I thought it odd that Pearl gave the engagement her blessing. I was confused and wondered if Paul,

Karl, Sam, and I had been totally wrong about Harris being gay and that he and Pearl shared a romantic relationship.

One day Clarissa brought her daughter, Naomi, to the office and introduced her to me. She was a freshman at American University in DC and had just arrived to spend the weekend at home. I was struck with her beauty: long brown hair, blue eyes, and sexy legs in her cute mini skirt. I figured her boyfriend was one lucky guy.

Naomi was very kind and tried to engage me in conversation, but I made a fool of myself because I couldn't seem to find my voice. I figured she thought of me as some kind of bumpkin, but, to her credit, she didn't. She saw something in me that she liked.

Clarissa suggested that I come to their house for lunch the next day. Harris encouraged me to get to know this family, which I readily agreed to. In fact, Naomi and I spent most of the weekend together. It wasn't long before I fell in love with her.

Of course, she had to return to school, but we stayed in touch by writing letters and calling. Whenever I could get away from Harris and Buck, I drove down to DC to see her.

Naomi showed me around numerous sites of the capital. She knew all the historical places to visit, the hip stores to shop, the best bars to eat and drink. We fit in with "the crowd."

One cold evening after a nice dinner and a few drinks, we drove out to the Lincoln Memorial. Fog was rolling in from the Potomac River. We climbed all the way to the top of the stairs and looked out over the impressive panorama of the National Mall. The memorial's lights shimmered in the reflecting pool that separated the Lincoln Memorial from the Washington Monument.

We walked into the memorial and stood before the statue of Lincoln. It's one thing to see the statue in pictures, but it's quite another to stand before it. We craned our necks to look into the face of this famous president.

Naomi told me to stand in front of the statue. She stepped down from the platform, turned to me, and raised her right hand. The fog in the wintery night framed the moment in my mind forever. Her warm breath came in puffs that reflected in the monument spotlights. "I hereby solemnly swear in the presence of Abraham Lincoln that I love Robert Park more than anyone in this world and that I will continue to love him until death do us part."

The beauty of the memorial faded, and I saw only Naomi. She was a vision standing before me in her navy overcoat, a gray knitted cap and matching gloves, eyes moist with tears, and lips smiling. My heart was light with joy.

I went to her. Before the Abraham Lincoln Memorial and in sight of the Washington Monument, we hugged and kissed and pledged our eternal love to each other.

We found a motel room and made love for the first time.

Though we kept our relationship quiet, Harris and Clarissa were moving forward with their wedding scheduled for December 7, 1968, Pearl Harbor Day. Invitations were sent out to the Foundation board members as well as the socialites of Philadelphia and New York. This marriage celebration was to be an extravaganza, so no detail was left to chance. The couple hired professionals to ensure a perfect wedding. The media was to play an integral part, which, of course, was designed to put the Foundation in the spotlight.

Clarissa was excited with the upcoming nuptial. Her joy couldn't be suppressed. It shone on her face every day.

Naomi had mixed feelings about the marriage. She wanted her mother to be happy, but she was unsure about Harris becoming her stepfather. Because of what I'd told her, she knew about Harris's affection toward Ms. Buck, his relationship with Jimmy Pauls, and the question of misuse of Foundation funds. She tried to be happy for her mother and went along with the flow of plans. But Clarissa could read her daughter's face and knew she wasn't fully on board with the marriage.

Instead of ignoring the accusations, Clarissa chose to learn more about Harris. Because I was close to Naomi, had been living at the Foundation, and traveled with Harris, she asked me many questions. I could not hide what I knew, so I answered them honestly while trying not to insert my opinion about Harris. It wasn't long before her smiles disappeared and her face showed serious concern.

One weekend before Thanksgiving of that year, and only a couple of weeks before Harris and Clarissa's wedding, Chuck, John, and I were called to the Hilltop House. While Chuck and John were sleeping upstairs, Harris kept me downstairs into the early morning hours to discuss Foundation business. He had been drinking heavily. His conversation took a strange turn, and he started to say some nonsensical stuff about how out of all the boys he loved me most and that I was his favorite. He said that because of his love for me he forgave me for betraying him.

I sensed where he was going with this and immediately put up my guard. He came toward me and hugged me. When he tried to kiss me on the lips, I pushed him away. But that didn't stop him. He again approached me, this time crying and begging.

At that moment, I realized I hated him. He was an

evil man who didn't care about me or the Amerasians. My insight became crystal clear. His favor toward me wasn't based on care or compassion but on infatuation and self-interest. He used me and the other boys as a pretense to fool Ms. Buck and the world into thinking how concerned he was about the plight of Amerasians. He lied, cheated, and manipulated to get whatever he wanted. We were simply victims of his machinations.

Rage blinded me to any possible consequences. I wanted to punch his face and beat him until my fury was satisfied. As he forced his way toward me, I brought up my fists and aimed for his face. At the last second, something within cautioned me against the violence I longed to inflict. I pulled my punch, but struck his right shoulder. I could cause him pain without getting myself into a lot of trouble.

He fell to the floor, screaming. Then he began yelling that he was going to die unless taken to the hospital. Awakened by the commotion, Chuck and John rushed downstairs. I hadn't known it at the time, but Jimmy Pauls was visiting. He seemed to show up out of nowhere.

Seeing Harris on the floor, crying like a baby, Pauls threatened me. Twice my size, he was a serious menace. I took a karate stance and challenged him to come on. I would fight him to the death if necessary. My face and posture must have convinced him of my intent, because he backed off and retreated.

I left the house and drove through New Hope to Yardley where Clarissa was living by the Delaware River. I told her what had just happened. This was the final straw for her. She decided to call off the wedding. She was devastated but knew it was the only thing to do.

Harris had no injury and did not seek medical care. But I knew him well enough to know what he was thinking: he had to figure a strategy to cover his actions. Even more so, he had to paint a picture of being the victim.

It would seem Pearl S. Buck had another crisis at hand.

The next day, Clarissa, Harris, and I went to see Pearl. Harris told her that I had become violent for no reason, and that I had beat him to the degree that his shoulders were permanently damaged. He went so far as to claim that even the bones may have been broken.

Then he turned on Clarissa, verbally attacking her by trashing her background. He wove a story about how she'd divorced her husband because she was involved with the civil rights movement with Dr. Martin Luther King Jr. (you'll recall that Ms. Buck didn't like him). He went on with his slander, saying she was not to be trusted with the Foundation work and that he fired her. However, the truth was that Clarissa had already resigned from her position and simultaneously canceled the wedding.

The uncanny thing of it all was that Pearl S. Buck, the literary genius, soaked up all his lies as truth and, in fact, joined in the nasty fight to preserve Harris's love for her and his position at the Foundation. She gave me a ruthless tongue-lashing and spread Harris's lies about me throughout the Foundation. In summary, she told the staff and the other Amerasians that I was a horrible person.

All these recent events jeopardized my future with the Foundation once again. In fact, my chance of surviving this recent character assassination was near zero. I had to do something if I was going to stay in the country and not face deportation.

I had met Dr. Wilson and his family in Korea when Pearl and Harris had last visited. He and his wife had hearts for the Amerasian children and became big donors for the Foundation. Subsequently, Harris also put him on the board. I called Dr. Wilson in Tucson, Arizona. He listened as I told him the sordid story. The man became concerned and invited me to Arizona. He bought me an airline ticket, so I quickly packed a bag and slipped out through the Foundation building's back door.

Chapter Ten

———◆———

EXPOSÉ

A SMALL CITY, TUCSON WAS HOT AND arid, just as it was portrayed in the Westerns I used to watch.

Dr. Wilson was a professor of geology at the University of Arizona. He and his wife ran the Robert T. Wilson Foundation, which Dr. Wilson had inherited from his father. The foundation helps provide education for poor children and supports efforts in the conservation of natural resources. In addition, Dr. Wilson had purchased a large Spanish-style house to host several Navajo and Apache Indian children, run by a family he hired from New Zealand.

He was a simple, humble, and kind-hearted man. You could never tell he was a multimillionaire by the way he dressed, talked, or acted. On one of the fund-raising trips I took with Harris and Ms. Buck, we had visited with Dr. Wilson and his wife. Impressed by the Foundation's work, he gave over $500,000 to the Pearl S. Buck Foundation and pledged an additional million dollars.

The Wilsons were hospitable and sympathetic to my plight. He counseled me to focus on my studies and not worry about the problems with the Foundation. He then enrolled me at the University of Arizona and set me up in a nice apartment near the campus. Studying was exactly what I focused on, and I got very good grades.

One day in April 1969, Clarissa called me and said that Greg Walter with *Philadelphia Magazine* was coming to Tucson to interview me. He'd heard a few rumors about the Foundation's misuse of funds, shady dealings, and, of course, had questions about Harris's involvement. As an investigative reporter on assignment, he was looking to dig up and expose all the dirt about the Foundation, and then write a sensational article.

Greg was a brilliant investigative writer who'd earned his reputation by exposing the shakedown schemes of another investigative reporter, Harry Karafin of the *Philadelphia Inquirer.* That article eventually led to Karafin's indictment and subsequent incarceration. Greg had also locked horns with the likes of Frank Rizzo (then a police commissioner and later the mayor of Philadelphia), Arlen Specter (then

District Attorney of Philadelphia and later US Senator representing Pennsylvania), and Richard Sprague (then Deputy District Attorney of Philadelphia). Greg was such a threat to suspected corrupt officials that when the police pulled a body from the Schuylkill River and thought it was his, the city coroner seized Greg's medical records to determine identification. I'm not sure if they ever identified the body, but I'm happy to report that it was not Greg.

At first I was hesitant to talk to him because Dr. Wilson had told me not to get involved in Foundation matters. But Clarissa eventually persuaded me, against my better judgment, to talk to the reporter. She said that Greg had been compiling information about Ted Harris and Pearl Buck for quite some time and would publish the article whether I cooperated or not. I feared that if I didn't give Greg my story and perspective, he might print something that wasn't quite true and put me in a bad light.

Had I known that Harris's betrayal of Clarissa had put her in a vindictive mindset and that Greg was paying her to help him, I would not have agreed to the interview or participated in the exposé. But because Clarissa and Greg withheld this information from me, I once again became the pawn in someone else's game.

Greg had graduated from Columbia and, as fate would have it, had attended a writers' workshop taught by Pearl S. Buck. By the time he'd come to see me, he had already interviewed her twice. Evidently their first session was pleasant and laid-back, but when he pressed her on Harris and his dealings, Buck told him, "You are vile. You were my favorite pupil, but now I am terribly disappointed and ashamed of you." She'd flung these same words at me when my friends and I went to report Harris's questionable activities to her.

Greg taped my four-hour interview. He said he was planning to publish the article in the July 1969 issue of *Philadelphia Magazine*. His strategy was to bombard the media with this exposé. Paul Rust, news director with WIP radio station in Philly, had also been working with Greg and was taping interviews with the Japanese and Korean Amerasians in the United States on scholarship from the Foundation. These interviews would be broadcast in five-minute segments every hour, beginning the day the magazine hit the stands. Greg wanted me to interview with Rust also.

I didn't give much thought to interviewing with Rust. Of course, Greg tried to talk me into it. He said that Rust had interviewed Sam, Paul, Karl, Chuck, and John. They felt betrayed and used by Ms. Buck when we'd gone to her to warn her of Harris's dealings, and she did nothing but punish us. So they felt compelled to uncover the corruption going on at the Foundation by telling the truth to the world. Greg tried to guilt-trip me into thinking that because my friends were doing this, I should support them and also interview with Rust. The bottom line was that I'd have to return to Philadelphia, something I wasn't willing to do.

Once Greg left, I shifted my focus back to my studies and successfully completed my first semester at the University of Arizona. Dr. Wilson got me a summer job at a geological research center, run by his brother, in the Flagstaff area. They gave me a small trailer to live in onsite, and I worked at various menial jobs.

The location was isolated. Other than a few security guards, the place was deserted at night. Loneliness once again took up residence within me.

My seclusion left me with too much time to think. I wondered how this problem with the Foundation would pan out on the East Coast. My greatest fear was for those Amerasians who would get caught in the crossfire and lose their financial help if the Foundation was forced to shut down.

I also thought about Naomi. How I missed her! Long-distance romances are difficult to manage under the best of conditions, but in the late '60s, we had no e-mail, Skype, or cell phones with unlimited calling, texting, or free long distance. Back then, we had to write letters and send them via snail mail, and since two thousand miles separated us, we had to pay dearly for long-distance calls. Letters and calls became fewer and farther between. I was feeling stuck in the wide open spaces of Arizona.

And then Naomi surprised me with a visit. Her mother, Clarissa, thought it would be helpful for Naomi and me to be together, so she bought Naomi's plane ticket. We took long walks and talked late into the night. We were both falling deeper in love.

A few days later, Naomi had to return home. It was too painful for me to say good-bye. I wanted to marry Naomi, so I decided to go back to Philadelphia with her. We called her mother to see if she would agree to this.

Of course, Clarissa was in full agreement. My returning to Philly was exactly what she and Greg hoped for. They believed I should be at ground zero when Greg's exposé exploded onto the newsstands in the next couple of weeks.

I packed my meager belongings and left a note at the center's personnel office. Naomi and I drove across the continent back to Philadelphia in less than two days.

As soon as I arrived in Philly, I met with Paul Rust and taped an interview, which was to be broadcast in a few days. And then I met up with Chuck and John. After a short discussion, we all decided that for the sake of the 50,000 Amerasians in Korea, the right thing to do would be to approach Ms. Buck one more time and warn her about Harris and the trouble he was bringing to the Foundation and to Ms. Buck herself. We believed there was still time to reverse the release of Greg's damaging article, halt the broadcast of our interviews, and thus save the Foundation. Of course, Harris and Ms. Buck were clueless as to Walter's investigation.

They were staying at the Chesapeake house Harris had convinced Pearl to buy sight unseen that day we were traveling back from DC. I knew the way, so I drove. The houses in this rural setting were spaced out. By the time we arrived, it was pitch-dark. The only sounds were chirping crickets and the gentle waves lapping against the shore. The salty air mixed with the sweet scent of freshly mowed grass and the exotic aroma of gardenias.

Before knocking on the door, we peeked through the window and saw Harris sleeping in the armchair, his mouth agape and a drink still in his hand. We moved to the front door and used the knocker.

Almost immediately, the interior lights flicked off. A booming voice reverberated through the closed door. "What do you want?"

I recognized Jimmy Pauls's voice.

"We want to talk to Miss Buck. It's important," I said.

Pauls hollered the vilest of curses and threatened to call the cops.

Chuck, John, and I knew we had to do something

quickly or we would be in trouble. Jimmy would certainly not hesitate to call the police.

I stood a few steps outside the entrance and raised my voice, hoping Pearl would hear me. "Ms. Buck, please talk to us. The Foundation and your reputation are at stake. We have never wanted to hurt you or the Foundation. You know how we care about the Amerasians. In a few days, the media is going to explode with revelations about Mr. Harris and all the wrongs he has done with the Foundation. Ms. Buck, I plead with you to listen to us. It's not too late to avert this crisis. All you have to do is to make changes. If you do, the press will not release their investigation. Please, listen to us! You have been deceived!"

I stopped. We waited. Within minutes we could hear Harris, Buck, and Pauls all talking. Of course, we couldn't hear what they were saying. So I pressed on with our pleas.

Jimmy evidently made good on his threat to call the police. I had barely resumed calling for Ms. Buck to come out and talk to us when speeding cars flashing bright blue, red, and white lights rushed toward us and screeched to a stop in the driveway. The sheriff emerged from the lead car and ordered us to stand away from the house and spread our legs with our hands on the hood of the cruiser.

As soon as we complied, a rush of deputies searched

us. I was thankful they didn't cuff us. We waited while the sheriff talked to Pearl, Harris, and Pauls, trying to determine the problem. Ms. Buck couldn't make up her mind about pressing charges against us for trespassing. Of course I wasn't privy to the conversations that took place between her and Harris and the sheriff, but she seemed unsure what to do about us. She kept going back and forth between Harris and the cops. In the end, she chose to press charges of trespassing, and she accused me of threatening Harris.

The sheriff said we'd all have to go down to the station. Chuck, John, and I were instructed to drive our car between the two cruisers. Ms. Buck rode in one of the police cars with the officers.

We entered the small station. The magistrate took me into a room and questioned me first. I told him what had been happening regarding the misuse of Foundation funds and the treatment by Harris. I told him about the upcoming release of the investigative article and radio interviews, which included serious allegations against Harris, Pearl, and the Foundation. I finished my explanation by telling him that we'd driven down to the house simply to warn Ms. Buck of the coming crisis, in hopes that she would take steps to protect herself and the Foundation.

He asked if we'd attempted to break into the house. We hadn't, so I said no; we had only knocked on the door and talked from outside the house.

He appraised me with a long look then seemed to decide I was telling the truth.

He escorted me back to the waiting area, where he addressed Ms. Buck. "I can lock these boys in jail, but by tomorrow morning the media will have access to the fact of their arrest. They will likely take a keen interest because you, a high-profile personality, have pressed charges. Those newshounds will latch onto this story like flies on honey, digging for every detail and sensationalizing this incident. And there's nothing I can do to stop it. So, do you want to press charges?"

Again, Ms. Buck wavered. I'm not sure why she seemed so conflicted. Did she worry about her reputation if what we said was true? Did she wonder about the Foundation's survival if any of it was true? Did she entertain doubts about Harris's integrity? I don't know her thoughts that night, but she clearly was not sure what she should do. She even asked the magistrate for his opinion. He, of course, declined to comment and pressed for her decision.

Whether to justify our actions or to cover herself— or Harris—Ms. Buck kept saying how misled we boys were, that we were troubled kids in Korea, and how she and Harris had given us a once-in-a-lifetime opportunity to study in the United States. The more she talked, the more she seemed to convince herself that Chuck, John, and I continually "made trouble and should be punished for attempting to break into the house and hurling threats at Harris, who, by the way, is the gentlest soul on earth."

It was difficult to listen to her talk like this. I had seen for myself how Harris used Foundation funds for his own pleasure. I had experienced his manipulations and sexual advances. He and Buck had used my name for an illegal property purchase in Korea. This information and more was about to hit the newsstands and airways. We had tried to warn her for her own sake, and yet she still saw Harris and herself as victims.

Eventually, likely out of fear of the media, Pearl withdrew her charges.

The sheriff told us to leave town immediately and never to return. Around 2:00 AM we began driving back to Philly. Chuck, John, and I were downhearted, since our honest intentions had not only been rejected but also distorted and used against us. But we believed we had done the right thing. Now all we could do was step back as the media bomb was about to explode.

Chapter Eleven

———•———

DEPORTATION

THE JULY 1969 ISSUE OF *PHILADELPHIA Magazine* dedicated twenty-one pages to the article by Greg Walter titled "The Dancing Master." It began with a full-page portrait of Ted Harris, followed by a smaller one of Pearl S. Buck with the subtitle "Famed novelist Pearl S. Buck has been waltzed into a heartbreaking story."

The article was so thorough, detailed, and documented that any dispute would be very difficult to substantiate. The article sparked a chain reaction in the media. All local newspapers, including the *Philadelphia Inquirer* and WIP AM radio, ran the news as headlines. Nationally, the July 25, 1969, issue of *Time* magazine reported the investigation by Greg Walter in the Press section under the heading "Crumbling Foundation":

> Daimler and Sapphires. As Walter tells it, Harris was a dancing instructor who, in 1963, wanted to

be just a gigolo and began ingratiating himself into the comfortable Bucks County life of Pearl Buck. He fawned, she loved it; together they wrote a mawkish book (For Spacious Skies) [sic] about finding one another. A year later, she made him president of the news foundation. He left his dance-studio job and moved into (rent free) the organization's elegant town house in Philadelphia's Delancey Place. Soon, writes Walter, Harris had collected "several thousand dollars worth" of suits, jewelry (he went for diamond and sapphire rings), an expensive Daimler automobile, credit cards, exotic birds, camera equipment. The Buck name drew well, and by 1965 the board of governors included Art Buchwald, Sargent Shriver and Mrs. William Scranton. The foundation prospered."

I was quoted also:

There was difficulty in getting one, Bob Park, out of Korea because he was of draft age. But Harris found him so attractive that he had Miss Buck pull strings. Park, now a student at the University of Arizona, remembers: "One night on the way to America he asked me about my father and I began to cry; he kissed me on the neck. When I would go to bed he would hold me in his arms. I did not like it, but I thought this was the way American father treat [sic] his son."

Then the inevitable happened: I was summoned to appear at the Immigration Department in downtown Philadelphia. In retaliation for the exposé, Ms. Buck was pulling her sponsorship of me and the other boys, thereby having us deported to Korea. I did not want to return to Korea. It was unfair for me to be punished for others' wrongdoing, but Ms. Buck's turning her back on me was just another in a string of similar rejections.

Fighting panic, I immediately notified Greg Walter, who was sympathetic but couldn't help me. My thoughts turned to the only other person who could help. I realized then that I had made a grave error in not heeding Dr. Wilson's advice to stay out of Foundation affairs, and I was ashamed for leaving Arizona as I had, because he and his wife had been good to me. But I didn't know who else to turn to for help. I called him and explained my situation.

He could have told me that I had been foolish in ignoring his wisdom. He could have said that I blew my chance with him because I'd left my job, which he'd gotten for me, without proper notification. He could have said I was on my own because he'd already helped me out of a mess. But that was not his way. He never said or even implied "I told you so." This kind man simply said, "I'll get you an attorney who will take you to the immigration office tomorrow morning and do everything possible to keep you in the States."

I have never been as grateful as I was right then. Dr. Wilson was a shining light in those dark days. I had no idea what would happen to me, and I feared being sent back to Korea, but his act of caring and kindness gave me hope.

I didn't sleep much the night before the hearing in the immigration office. The weather that morning seemed fitting for what I was about to face: hot, steamy, and oppressive. As I approached the office building, about a dozen press members were waiting at the front entrance. They held notebooks, cameras, and microphone extensions. Of course, I didn't know why they were there or whom they were waiting for, but I figured something big must be happening, some newsworthy activity at Immigration.

Imagine my horror when they spotted me, rushed forward, and peppered me with questions. I was totally taken by surprise and unprepared.

"Is Pearl Buck's love affair with Harris true?"

"Did you actually witness that?"

"Did she have sex with him?"

"Is Harris homosexual?"

"Did he really bring you boys for homosexual purposes?"

"Is it true that the Foundation is run by a gang of homosexuals?"

The questions flew at me, no one waiting for me

to answer before another reporter flung a question. Which was a good thing, because I didn't know where to begin, if at all. My thoughts spun. I had to go inside to keep the appointment, but I also didn't want to miss the opportunity to let the world know what happened. Right then, the attorney sent by Dr. Wilson came to my rescue and handled the reporters.

"Before we answer any questions, Mr. Park and I will meet with officials to learn why Miss Buck notified the Immigration Department. Then my client and I will meet with the press and answer questions."

He escorted me into the office, where the immigration official introduced himself. He seemed nervous with all the media attention, so he was rather brief. He read the letter from Buck, which stated she was withdrawing her sponsorship because I was not studying as I should have, and that I was being influenced to stir up trouble in our country. She requested that I be deported immediately. The official noted that I had thirty days to find another sponsor if I wanted to remain in the country.

Ms. Buck had written this same letter concerning Chuck and John, asking that they also be deported.

Like faithful dogs, or annoying colds, the press had not grown impatient in waiting. Instead, they had camped out in a conference room. The attorney gave them a brief statement and said he had no further comments. He also said I would not answer any questions. This shocked me.

I whispered in his ear, "I want to speak. They must know the truth."

"No way, Bob. Dr. Wilson said that for your protection, we should not speak to the press and not answer any questions."

You'd think I would have learned to take the counsel of Dr. Wilson. Well, I didn't. I could not agree to keep quiet. I figured I might never have another chance like this if I were sent back to Korea.

I stepped in front of the attorney and faced the press. The cameras clicked and bulbs flashed. I cleared my throat. "All the facts recorded in Walter's article in the *Philadelphia Magazine* are true and correct. We tried to save the Foundation by alerting Miss Buck on several occasions, but she has stubbornly refused to face up to the truths and has instead defended Mr. Harris. In the meantime, thousands of honest and loving Americans are sending in their hard-earned monthly donations, which are wasted and squandered by Ted Harris and his gang. I do not want to destroy the Foundation or Miss Buck's fame, because I and my friends care so much about the Amerasians who need help. But today, Miss Buck put all the blame on me, Chuck, and John and ordered us deported for telling the truth. It is obvious that she desires to continue this deceptive management of the Foundation and its cover-up."

And then, to my attorney's horror, I agreed to take questions from the press. The session lasted about an hour, and all the local TV channels carried the news that evening. The newspapers also continued to carry the story, but, unfortunately, it was shrouded by the greater news that Apollo 11 with Neil Armstrong had landed on the moon for the first time in human history.

Chapter Twelve

———•———

DESERTER

REV. GILBERT HORN, A TALL AND HANDSOME Presbyterian minister in Perkasie, followed the news stories about the Foundation. He became concerned about the welfare of us Amerasian boys and persuaded some members of his congregation to become sponsors for us in place of Pearl Buck. At least that allowed us to remain in the country.

I had moved in with Clarissa and Naomi Brown in Yardley. Of course, this was an ideal arrangement for Naomi and me. Adding to my delight was Naomi's decision to take a semester off school and stay in Yardley.

Rev. Horn helped me enroll in Bucks County Community College. Once again, peace and quiet in my life allowed me to focus on my studies.

John was placed with the Roberts family in Perkasie, a quintessential family. The parents and the three children accepted John into their lives and legally adopted him. Mrs. Dana Roberts impressed me with her kindness and generosity. She seemed to be the perfect wife and mother: good-looking, loving, hardworking. She even gave us English lessons during the summer months. It was easy to respect her.

I was happy that John had found his loving forever family and that he was truly a son and a brother. He had grown up in an orphanage and never knew what it was like to be part of a family. Not only was he grateful for their bigheartedness, but also he was excited to be counted among them.

For the first time in quite a while, I felt all was right with my world.

I should have known it wouldn't last.

Dana began confiding in Clarissa that all was not well between herself and her husband. Theirs was a troubled relationship. Then I learned the most shocking thing: Dana and John were having an intimate relationship.

I couldn't believe it. It was too bizarre. Yet it was true.

If that weren't enough, I learned that John tried to lure Naomi into seeing him—all behind my back, of course.

These things in quick succession thrust me into bewilderment. I had put my trust in Pearl Buck, but she betrayed me. I had put my trust in the Roberts family, but Mrs. Roberts and John betrayed me. I trusted John as a friend, but he betrayed me. And I hated him from that point. These events served to force me to reassess my nature. I trusted people too easily.

I just wanted to live my life in America in peace. I wanted to study, to marry one day and have a family. I wanted a normal, contented life. I wanted to leave the past behind me and move on.

To be honest, I couldn't help but follow the news concerning the Foundation. I certainly did not want it to fail, because I cared about the many Amerasians who were receiving help from the Foundation. Nor did I want Ms. Buck's reputation ruined. But I certainly did not want Harris to get away with his selfish, underhanded, and possibly illegal deeds. I eventually concluded that the Foundation couldn't continue under the present structure of corruption.

According to the press, Harris had resigned his position at the Foundation and retreated to Buck's estate in Vermont. The District Attorney of Pennsylvania initiated an investigation into the Foundation's solicitation methods and use of its funds. Pearl Buck, not long after this, was diagnosed with lung cancer. She and Harris, a chain smoker, usually had spent more than eighteen hours a day together, and I don't recall them ever being separated, even for a day. So though Ms. Buck didn't smoke, I wondered if all the secondhand smoke she'd breathed had caused her cancer.

It seems to me that by allowing Harris into her life and work, she opened herself to irreparable damage to both her health and her good name. She seemed to have remained blind to the destruction he wrought in so much of the good she established in her life, because at her death in 1973, she apparently left most of her assets to Harris. Her adopted daughters challenged this provision in her will and recovered most of it through lengthy legal battles.

But simply being away from the Foundation and not being drawn into the activities and dealings of it, I enjoyed a measure of peace. But, as usual, it was short-lived.

In the spring of 1970, President Park, the dreaded dictator of Korea, summoned all draft-age students studying overseas to return and complete their military obligation. To set an example, he first focused on the sons of his cabinet members. Eventually, I received my notice to return. The Korean Embassy in DC was instructed not to extend our passports.

Dr. Wilson couldn't help me this time. I was on my own. I had to decide between two possibilities: go back to Korea and serve in the wretched army, or join the US Army and be shipped off to Vietnam. If I joined the

US Army, I would also receive US citizenship. Chuck and John had quickly chosen the only option that made sense to them: the US Army and citizenship. By the time I received my notice to report back to Korea, they were finishing up their basic training.

Naomi, heavily involved in the anti-war movement both on and off campus, was beside herself when I concluded that the no-brainer choice was to join the US Army. The war in Vietnam was at its peak. Despite his campaign promises, Richard Nixon didn't seem anywhere near ending the war. If I did return to Korea and join the army, I'd still be sent to Vietnam, because they were in there fighting too. Whether I stayed in the United States or returned to Korea, I would be going into the army and fighting in Vietnam. It simply came down to deciding between armies.

So it was a lonely way to Fort Bragg, North Carolina, and a lonely eight weeks in basic training. On the day of graduation, I looked on others with envy as their parents, girlfriends, and relatives attended the ceremony. Because of her stance against the war, Naomi refused to be there.

I was commissioned to go to Fort Polk, Louisiana, for the ten-week jungle training, where I would be groomed for combat in Vietnam. The training was arduous and never ending. The soaring temperatures, along with high humidity, mosquitoes, and poison ivy added to my daily misery. As expected, I received my orders for Vietnam. I was given a ten-day leave before I had to report for duty. I went to Yardley to be with Naomi.

While I was in basic training and sweating in the swamps of Louisiana, Naomi had contacted an anti-war group at Princeton that had directed her to an expat group in Toronto, Canada. This was a community of war resisters who'd emigrated from the United States. Because I had no money to get to Canada and set up housekeeping once I'd arrived, she even arranged a $300 loan from Dr. Mario Copecchi of Harvard (he would be awarded a Nobel Prize in 2007), whom we had befriended. Canada did not fight in the Vietnam War, and its policy made it relatively easy for deserters, draft dodgers, and other resisters to enter the country. At this point, 50,000 deserters and draft-dodgers had emigrated from the United States to Canada.

On the day I was to head for San Francisco, where I would then be shipped to Vietnam, I took a bus to Toronto.

Chapter Thirteen

———•———

MINER

I DIDN'T REMAIN IN TORONTO LONG BECAUSE I couldn't find work. American expats referred me to their branch in Ottawa. There they'd help me find a job and apply for permanent residency. So I hopped another bus and headed northeast to Ottawa.

It was September 1, 1970, and the streets of Ottawa bustled with students starting the new school year. The weather had suddenly turned cool, with autumn arriving early. I had $50 in my pocket and a small bag that held my meager belongings—but no winter coat.

I missed Naomi like crazy. We wrote to each other almost daily. She visited once, and it was during our time together that we both sensed we were drifting apart. I couldn't return to the United States because I was a deserter and would be arrested once on US soil, and she had become more politically radical. Eventually, we would recognize that our long-distance relationship wasn't enough for either of us. When she returned home, we continued to exchange letters, but they became a mere trickle and then dried up completely.

My French-Canadian landlord was anything but a friend. He was ruthless and had a foul mouth. I knew my days were numbered in the small room I rented from him. He would throw me out to the street if I did not find a job quickly. Every day I combed the newspaper Help Wanted ads—as did the other 50,000 immigrants looking for work.

Then I saw an ad that caught my eye. The International Nickel Company was hiring miners in Sudbury, Ontario. The only requirement was good physical health and a minimum body weight of 170 pounds. This would be my risk-all attempt for survival. I took the long bus ride to the mining city, with no assurance that I would land the job.

But I did. The nature of the employment—working with explosives—generated a high turnover rate.

My first assignment was with the blasting crew 3500 feet underground. Though minimal, my experience with handling explosives in the army helped me obtain this dangerous but high-paying job. I made $3.75 an hour when the average wage at the time was a little over $1.50. But like all towns that sprang up around booming mines throughout history, the cost of living was ridiculously high. Even at that, I was able to buy an old station wagon for $100 and save a big portion of my income.

Accidents in the mines were common. I thought of my buddies in Vietnam and took small comfort that I was also fighting for survival in a hazardous environment. This was my feeble effort to cover the guilt I felt for not going to war.

One day I did come close to death. My team members with twenty-plus years of seniority were blown apart in a blasting accident. I survived only because they'd ordered me to stand guard and block anyone from entering while they went to check the area we had dynamited. Their fatal mistake was in hurrying. It was nearing the end of our graveyard shift, and they wanted to make it to the shaft elevators without delay. Instead of waiting the full fifteen minutes after detonation to allow for slow-burning fuses to ignite, they went in after about eight minutes. Their years of experience told them it was safe, but little did they know that a fuse was still burning, and a few sticks of dynamite remained undetonated. Three miners died that day. Only their lunch pails made it to the surface and were handed over to their widows.

I could not erase the image in my mind of the despairing widows accepting the meager remains of their loved ones. It seemed their human dignity and experiences summed up to no more than the value of those lunch pails. What if it had been me? Is my life worth that little? Just the thought of dying like that in this northern country so far from my mother and girlfriend both saddened and scared me.

Questions arose within me. What happens after you die? Is there such a thing as heaven as I'd heard some Christians talk about? How about hell? Who goes there? Who and what will decide one's fate? I had no answers to these troubling questions.

Looking out my little window, against which the winter snowstorms beat, I stayed awake all night. At times it would snow enough to bury my car parked on the street. Travel in such deep snow was impossible, and I couldn't make it to work. The temperature would sometimes drop to thirty below zero. Just being stuck in my little room forced me to ask these essential questions of life and death.

I visited a bookstore and found several books I thought would provide some answers. I did a lot of reading. (What else could I do on those long and snowy winter nights?) I read books on Buddhism, Taoism, and Confucianism but never about the Christian faith or the Bible. I also read such books as *Crime and Punishment* and *The Brothers Karamazov* by Dostoevsky, *Demian* and *Steppenwolf* by Hermann Hesse, and several of Hemingway's titles. But these books cast more shadow upon the clouds of my mind. I tried to shake it off by hanging around night clubs, but nothing seemed to chase away these haunting questions.

In retrospect it was a miracle that no one ever tried to offer their views or religious beliefs to me. Ultimately, I decided to put my unanswered questions on the back burner and move on with my life.

After thirteen months of working in the mines, I moved to Toronto to go back to college. There I met Sue, who later would become my wife.

Sue had grown up in a solidly committed Christian family who faithfully attended church. She had long black hair and classic Korean looks and features. She played the guitar and sang the kind of songs I was very much into at the time.

Ever since I met the missionary in Daejeon—the one who promised me a pencil if I'd follow him to church—I carried with me a vague mental picture of Jesus. Could God have placed that image in my heart, or was it there because of my brief exposure to the gospel through that man? I don't know. I didn't know much about who Jesus was. I knew He died a painful death on the cross, though I didn't understand why and what it meant that He died for me. I also learned that He came back to life, was still living, and loved me very much. However limited my knowledge, it stuck with me.

I sought Him only in crises, like when I took the entrance exam to high school, or when I was sick or lonely. It seemed He sometimes came through and helped me, but other times He seemed absent.

Once, when I was a sophomore in high school, a group of five classmates took me to the back of the bathroom building, which was separated from the main building, and mercilessly beat me up. Their reasoning was that I was too arrogant and they simply didn't like me. But I suspected it was more than that—likely it was racially motivated.

When I came home with a bruised face and bloody nose, Mom cried. It angered and frustrated her that she could do nothing to stop these incidents or rectify them. Back then, teachers never interfered in these kinds of events. Unable to resolve the injustice, I was distressed and disappointed, and I questioned why Jesus wasn't there to help me. As a result, I concluded that He might not exist and dismissed my belief of Him as a figment of my imagination.

I did more than dismiss Jesus in high school. I despised some of my Christian classmates. I often ridiculed them along with my friends. Though I can't fully say why I did this, I can offer a couple of good guesses. First, I probably wanted to show how tough I was (which I wasn't), and, second, that I was a man. Actually, I was being a typical foolish teenage boy.

But I believe the deeper reason was because Christians were a minority—probably fewer than 10 percent of the population at the time. Because they rarely reacted to mocking and other abuses, I saw them as easy targets to pick on. I was unconsciously doing the things that were done to me—a pecking order.

Yet occasionally and secretly I thought of Jesus. But because I longed for the anti-Christian boys' acceptance, I hung around with them and followed their lead in picking on Christians.

The big questions of life haunted me: Is there a God? Who is Jesus? What happens after death? Are there ghosts? (I had heard many ghost stories when I was a kid, and I was scared of them.) I also struggled with the existence of evil in the world. Most of the books, movies, and stories I had been exposed to seemed to reinforce the concept that good wins over evil. But my reality failed to validate this. As far as I could see, the good based on truths or morals seemed powerless against evil people like Ted Harris, Jimmy Pauls, my stepfather, and many others.

Hindsight leads me to believe that God continued to prepare my heart by sending me to Canada, my "wilderness experience." When I worked in the mines, I was cut off from just about everyone and experienced acute loneliness and abandonment. People in Sudbury were cold, like the weather, and self-seeking. There was no place for me. I was afraid of death, and I felt it was waiting for me at the door. The fatalities of the miners further confirmed that fear. The only way to allay the fear was to know the truth about life after death. But where could I find the truth I so desperately longed for? I struggled with this almost day and night with no solution in sight.

By the time I met Sue, I had sort of buried my struggles and questions, though they were still with me. I knew she was a Christian, but I didn't want to ask her for help. I wrongly thought she would see that as weakness.

She wisely sought balance in introducing me to faith while not damaging our relationship. She bought me a copy of *The Living Bible* while attending a Christian conference in Chicago. I was grateful for the gift. At first I started reading in Genesis. You start reading all books at the beginning, right? From page one? You guessed it; I quickly got bored and dismissed the book as a myth or fairy tale.

A few days later, Sue gently inquired how I was doing with the book. When I told her exactly how I felt about it, she quickly realized her mistake in not telling me to read from the Gospels, preferably John.

So I tried again. How refreshing to read John's gospel! It was different from Genesis and far more interesting. Right from the start, the apostle wrote about Jesus. The information about Him and His sayings and teachings filled in the many blanks in my thinking about Jesus. As I read, He came alive to me, and I began to like Him a lot.

Most important was His assurance of life after death. "I am the way, truth and life" was my *aha* moment. The light bulb went on. My epiphany. I had been seeking the truth that I could hang my life on, and here He said that He is the Truth. I had been seeking the way and had thought it would be some kind of spiritual road map or how-to list or some hidden secret. But He said *He* is the Way: a person—God—not some theory or philosophy.

I fell in love with Jesus when I read of His suffering and crucifixion. I felt the magnitude of His love for me. I was a sinner whose goal was simply to survive. He bore the burden of my sins and paid the price to make me His own. Now I realized my life was worth a whole lot more than mere survival.

I thought back on all who had brought pain and misery to my life. Those things now seemed trivial and insignificant compared with what Jesus had undergone for me. The weight of my sins was greater than all acts of brutality toward me, than all derogatory and mean-spirited words slung at me. Jesus forgave me of every sin.

It was then that I forgave those who had hurt me.

I forgave the Koreans. I forgave John. I forgave Pearl Buck, Ted Harris, and Jimmy Pauls. I forgave my stepfather and my father, who had deserted Mother and me.

I felt free and light with my burdens lifted. I was on cloud nine as I felt loved and accepted.

The morning sun was just peeking over the eastern horizon when I finished reading the last chapter of John. I knelt by the window and prayed:

Jesus, how I thank You for loving me. Thank You for making me realize that You have been with me all these years, even when I was hurting and lonely and no one seemed to care. You have been with me even when I didn't know You. But Your loving hands have always protected me and led me this far. I invite You to take ownership of my life. I submit my life to You so that You may use me for whatever pleases You. Please help me to know You more, and teach me Your ways.

As I sat there with tears pouring down my cheeks, my nose running like a broken faucet, peace and joy and warmth infused my whole being. I didn't want it to end because it felt so good. Even in my newborn state, I knew it had to be the presence of my Lord.

I fell in love with Jesus and Sue at the same time.

I was transformed.

Chapter Fourteen

HOUSTON BOUND

My mother, stepfather, and half sister immigrated to America in 1974. They settled in Houston because my mother wanted to be closer to her nieces, who had been living there for many years. Since we lived on the same continent now, we could finally see each other. Having broken the law by becoming a deserter, I could not go to the United States without risking arrest, so in December 1975, Mom and Yuni were going to fly to Toronto to attend my wedding. After eight years of separation, we would be together. It was difficult to contain my anticipation.

My excitement about seeing my mother did not last long after her arrival. I couldn't help but notice a change in her. She seemed reserved, almost withdrawn. The joy that was her trademark appeared to have long disappeared from her face.

It was just before Christmas, and the weather was

unusually frigid and snowy. Mom complained about the weather, the food, my apartment, and more. But she was troubled the most by my intention to marry Sue. Mom openly criticized everything about her and continually pressured me to consider marrying someone she knew in Korea. Numerous times she pulled out a picture of a beautiful girl who could have passed as a model. She pointed to it and said this woman was from a wealthy family and would bring a substantial sum of money as dowry. (By then the Korean view toward half Koreans had somewhat loosened.)

You can probably imagine how this demeaned Sue. She had been looking forward not only to meeting my mother but also to being welcomed into the family. My mother's obvious disapproval deflated all the excitement and anticipation that had been building prior to her arrival. And not only that, her displeasure with Sue cast a tense pall on what should have been a joyous celebration. Mom refused to congratulate us on our upcoming wedding, much less bless us.

Despite my mother's opposition, Sue and I were joyfully married.

I had majored in business administration at Ryerson University in Toronto and began my career with a finance company, also in Toronto. Sue and I purchased a house in Mississauga, a suburb of Toronto and bought a small gift shop, which Sue operated on

Yonge Street. As a young couple, we were the envy of others. But one thing continued to bother me—my mother's refusal to accept my wife.

Things were not good between my mother and stepfather. I invited her to come and live with us, but she remained in Houston. Although I wouldn't fully understand until later, I knew she felt betrayed by me, her only son.

My stepfather was a self-educated and self-made man. But he also knew his limitations, which made him feel just insecure enough to compare himself with my mother's quality education and intelligence. He could not compete with her because even their friends recognized that she was smarter than he was. In his eyes, he came up short, and he was not happy about it. To compensate for this, he evidently felt he needed to deal with my mother's superior intellect by trying to make her dependent on him for everything—even trivial things. For example, he wanted her to rely on him even for her transportation. But Mom would not be outdone, so she took driving lessons, bought an old car, and started to drive on her own.

In Korea, my stepfather had worked as a criminal investigator for the Korean Police Department. Because he spoke fluent English, the US Army hired him at the end of the Korean War to work in the Criminal Investigation Department (CID) in Seoul. He worked for them for twenty years and was offered a chance to collect his retirement and receive his green card upon arriving in America.

He sold the house in Seoul, which my mother had originally purchased and paid for, pocketed the money, moved with Mom and Yuni to Houston, and started collecting his pension.

Once in the States, my stepfather did a lot of research and concluded that the only way he could get a decent job at his age and with his foreign background was to take courses to become an air conditioning specialist. This was far from the criminal investigation he was used to doing in Korea, but he always believed he could accomplish anything by setting clear, logical goals then putting in the effort. So he studied, took the state exam, received his license as a stationary engineer, and landed a job with Exxon.

Yet he still felt threatened by Mom. This kind of competition is not healthy for any relationship. If not stopped, it can take on a hostile edge, which happened in the case of my mother and her husband. He manipulated her and made her feel inadequate. He became an expert in emotional abuse.

He was about fifty-five and had plans for his life in America—and they didn't include my mother. His fatal blow to her was divorce. He took all the money and found a younger woman.

The shock and disappointment were too much for my mother. She grew insecure in this foreign land and did not know who else to turn to except her son in Canada, although reluctantly because of Sue.

When she first told me what my stepfather had done, I became furious. It brought up my old distrust of my stepfather. And his actions validated my feelings. I decided I needed to meet him face-to-face.

By then, President Jimmy Carter had declared amnesty for draft dodgers and deserters, so I flew to Houston. I met my stepfather at Winchell's Donut Shop on Beechnut Street. I tried to reason with him about an amicable divorce and dividing up the assets, including his savings and pension. He didn't appreciate my "interference" and immediately became irate. He denied having any money and cussed me out.

At that moment, all the memories of his mistreatment of me from the time I was little flashed in my mind. Anger swelled and threatened to take control—or rather hurl me out of control.

As he raised his voice, several customers stopped eating and stared at the growing hostility between my stepfather and me. Others hustled their children out, casting worried looks over their shoulders. Mom's husband was making a public display of the fool he was. He continued his agitated rant, peppering it with choice foul language.

As strong as the battle was brewing between the two of us, another deeper battle had begun within me. As a Christian, I knew that uncontrolled anger could lead to serious mistakes and actions. The old Bob wanted to punch out this guy's lights. And my deep-seated training in Asian culture niggled at the back of my mind, the part that forbids you from hurting someone older than you. But truth be told, I wanted him to throw the first punch. At least that way I'd be justified in using self-defense—and I'd have plenty of witnesses to back me up.

But he didn't strike me; instead, he stomped out of the store. We yelled at each other that we would "see you in court!"

Upon returning to my mother's home, I gave her the highlights of our "discussion." She was so stressed that she did not want to fight for what was rightfully hers. She didn't want to prolong what she saw as the inevitable; she just wanted it over. As she had always done, she made concession after concession. The result was that my now ex-stepfather had to pay only $150 per month in child support for Yuni. Mom got the house . . . and the mortgage. Her ex-husband got everything else, right down to the lawnmower.

Now my mother and sister were left in my care. They had no one but me to depend on. Of course, there was never any question in my mind that I would step into this role and do everything humanly possible for my family. But how? Toronto was 1500 miles from Houston. I couldn't just pop down there whenever the house needed a repair or Mom needed help with any number of things that could go wrong. The only solution was for her and Yuni to move to Toronto to live with Sue and me.

Mom and I went round and round over this issue. The bottom line was that Mother was adamant about staying in Houston. She would not concede. (Why couldn't she have been this stubborn when my stepfather was taking everything that was rightfully hers?)

Unable to change her mind, I had no choice but to return home—alone. I arrived at the Houston airport, checked in, and boarded the plane. All the while thoughts about how I could take care of Mom and Yuni while living so far away swirled through my head. Settled in my seat in the Toronto-bound airplane while it was waiting to take off on the runway, I forced my spirit to stillness and began praying—something I should have done right away, but I'm sure you've experienced similar situations. We fret and worry and try to figure out what to do. Finally, we realize we have no answers, so we turn to the Lord for help. Of course, He's always there, just waiting for us to calm down and look to Him for our needs.

So as the plane's engines thrummed as we taxied, I

prayed. "Lord, I don't know how to take care of Mom and Yuni. She refuses to move to Toronto. How can I possibly be of any use to her?"

A funny thing happened. The Lord spoke to me: *I want you to move here. I have a plan for you in this city.*

Did I hear that right? I asked God for a solution, and *bam!* He gives it. Did I fall on my knees, thanking Him? Stick with me; I know you've argued with God a time or two because you didn't get the answer you wanted.

"But, Lord, Sue and I are just now settled in Toronto. Her family is all there, and she's pregnant. How about my career? I'm beginning to move up the ladder. And what about the new house and the business we just bought? They won't be easy to sell."

God had every right to offer me some cheese to go with my whine, but He didn't. Instead He simply said, *Trust me.*

I knew in theory I could trust Him. I had read in the Bible of all His faithful acts concerning His people. And I was maturing in my Christian walk, learning from other believers how God worked in their lives and how He demonstrated His trustworthiness to them. But could I trust Him in this major life change?

When I arrived in Toronto, my nerves went to work. I was going to have to tell Sue that the Lord directed me to move to Houston. How would Sue respond to moving away from her loving family and near her mother-in-law, who barely registered her existence?

I knew I had an uphill battle ahead of me . . . and not just in convincing Sue to move. There was my work to consider, as well as selling our home and business— too many things had to happen all at once to make the move possible. Of course, Sue's pregnancy, the plans for the baby she and her mom were excitedly making, and her forty-plus relatives in Toronto were huge considerations. So before opening my mouth, I got smart and went to my knees. I put all the needs before God, and I asked Him to prepare Sue's heart.

After much thought and prayer, I finally talked to Sue and explained the situation with Mom and Yuni. Being full Korean, she understood the cultural dictate of my responsibility to my mother. We talked about the implications of moving to the United States and all that would require of us. And we couldn't ignore the reality that Sue would be leaving her family behind, just when they were anticipating the birth of their grandchild.

It was a lot to throw at my wife all at once. As usual, she did not get excited or upset or even throw a thousand questions at me. She just gave me the silent treatment. But not the kind you might be thinking. Whenever she goes silent, she's not locking me out because she's angry with me; instead, she goes silent so she can think and ponder and pray. It's as if she goes inside herself and finds her prayer closet within.

After spending a few days "within," Sue went to her mother and told her all that had taken place with my mother while I was in Houston, as well as what the Lord had told me to do about it. My mother-in-law is a very loving person, but far above this, she is a prayer warrior. Back in Korea, she spent many months on prayer mountains. Fasting and praying was a regular part of her spiritual routine. With decisions such as this, she relied on prayer.

We asked other people to pray for us, to help us determine with certainty that moving to Houston was, indeed, God's will for Sue and me. After a few days of sustained prayer, everyone who had joined and supported us in prayer unanimously concluded that it was God's will for us to move to Houston. Also, it was undisputed that no one liked the idea, but God's plans are sometimes like that.

Acting on what we knew to be the right course of action, we started to liquidate everything. We didn't think we'd have too much trouble selling our house, but our business was something else. Sometimes a business can sit on the market for a year or more, waiting for the one person out of countless who hears about it, wants it, and has the funds to purchase it. But when God has a plan, He can bring together any number of "odds" to accomplish His will.

And that's what He did for us. Within three months,

we had sold the house, the business, and most of our personal items. What we didn't sell, we gave away. In September 1980, we loaded our Buick with our few personal possessions, said tearful good-byes to my in-laws and our friends, and headed south.

We also prayed for a smooth drive all the way to Houston—a very good idea, since we would be crossing an international border.

While driving down Highway 401 toward Windsor, the southernmost city in Canada, we praised the Lord for using us for His purpose. What an honor and blessing to be part of God's work. Though Sue was "great with child," the joy of moving to our Promised Land overpowered her discomfort.

The joy did not last long as we faced our first obstacle on this long journey.

At the border crossing, the customs officer asked, "Where are you going?"

"We're moving to Houston to be with my mother."

"What is your nationality?"

"I am an American citizen, and my wife is Canadian."

"Ma'am, do you have a green card?"

"No, I don't. But I thought Canadians are allowed to live in the US."

Wrong.

Oops, my mistake. She is allowed to *visit* but not

live there. The officer sent us back to Canada.

He alerted us to another problem on the Canadian border. Because I didn't have my residency card, they would think I was trying to move from the United States to live in Canada illegally. I had to show ample proof that this was not the case. Once I showed my Canadian driver's license, my business card, and my Social Insurance card, they would let me pass. But Sue's lack of a green card would bar her from entering the United States.

We were devastated and even wondered if we might have read God wrong. Had I missed God's will? Would we ever make it to the States? What would happen to Mother and Yuni if we didn't get to Houston? What about Sue and our baby?

It was already getting dark, so we checked into a motel in Windsor, Ontario. We had to put our heads together.

First, we knelt on the floor and prayed. "Father God, You are almighty and holy, and we surrender our lives to You. We are still here in Canada and something is blocking our way to Houston. We believe we are following Your will, and that nothing can stop that. So we ask You to remove this obstacle or give us the wisdom to handle this situation."

Right then a thought came to me. Ten years prior, when traveling by bus, I crossed the border from

Buffalo, New York, into Canada. The officer only spot-checked some passengers. The questions they asked were very simple. In fact, when he came to me, the officer asked me a question then answered it himself. "Where are you going?"

"Toronto," I said.

"To check out the University of Toronto? It's a very good school—very popular with the Americans. In fact, my son goes there and enjoys it a lot. You'll like it."

I didn't have to say one word.

So the next morning, I put Sue on a Greyhound bus bound for Detroit. It should be an easy crossing, because it's not unusual for Canadians to cross the border to shop in Detroit. Once there, she would call and confirm she had crossed the border. I would then drive to the Detroit bus station and meet her.

After seeing her off, I kept praying, though I admit to being nervous. I didn't like her having to do this on her own, and there was always the thought that they'd pull her off the bus at the border. The wait seemed eternal.

And then the call finally came. "Honey, I made it! Praise the Lord. I'm here at the bus station. Come and get me!"

Hearing her voice released all the knots that had tightened every muscle in my body. I thanked the Lord all the way to Detroit.

It seemed as though Sue and I had been apart for ages, although less than two hours had passed from the time I put Sue on the bus until we were reunited.

We resumed praising the Lord while driving the endless highways all the way to Houston. I couldn't help but think how Mother would appreciate the sacrifices we had made and the obstacles we had to overcome just to be with her. Surely her heart would be ready to accept Sue and for us to present the gospel. A beautiful scenario played through my mind as I imagined how she would tearfully receive the Lord into her heart.

Had we known what was waiting for us in Houston, we would have seriously considered turning our Buick around and heading straight back to Toronto.

Chapter Fifteen

THE LETDOWN

MY MOTHER EXHIBITED SIGNS OF AN abused woman. I didn't think she was physically abused, but there was no question that her ex-husband had verbally, emotionally, and mentally mistreated her. She displayed all the classic signs, including being overly sensitive, lacking self-respect, thinking life (and everyone around her) was unfair toward her, moaning about not being able to depend on anyone (particularly me and Sue), while heaping unrealistic expectations upon us. If that were not enough, she suffered (and we along with her) mood swings, from self-pity to anger to remorse.

My mom's condition put a damper on the purpose of our coming to Houston, like a wet blanket on a fire. Though Sue and I talked to Mom about Jesus, she let us know that she wasn't interested and shut us up. We were stressed with trying to deal with Mom's erratic behavior. When she made excessive demands that I pay for her car repairs, medical expenses, groceries, and even provide her an allowance, I had to try to reason with her that Sue and I had limited finances. But that only triggered her negative feelings about Sue.

She never hid her animosity for her daughter-in-law. She still didn't think I should have married Sue. It became unbearable when Mom used harsh language toward Sue, and my little sister joined in. The bottom line was that she was jealous of my love for my wife.

Mom never acknowledged, much less showed any appreciation for, the sacrifices we made to be close to her so we could help her. It seemed she tried everything to make our lives miserable. And she was succeeding.

At first I tried to be patient, but my short supply ran out fast. I began to resent her inconsiderate attitude toward Sue and me. I always assumed she loved me, but now doubts crept in. I became angry. Instead of controlling it or seeking counsel on how to deal with my mother, I let my temper take over. I responded to her violently—not physically but certainly emotionally. I yelled and screamed and threatened to cut off the relationship and withdraw my support. I was becoming my stepfather!

Sue's reaction was the opposite of mine—and hers was a far more mature and loving one. She remained calm, even when being demeaned and used by my mother. She was compassionate and patient.

Looking back, I now realize I should have taken Mom to counseling. It would have helped me to understand the damage done to her self-respect and how she viewed herself. Counseling would also have equipped us to handle our relationship better.

Sue and I had to think about how we would make a living. We learned about a deli that was for sale. We took all the money we had brought from Canada and invested it in this new venture. We also gave the owners a note for the balance, payable within a year.

But the business did not do well, and soon we ran out of cash. We had to do something—fast.

I remember the day. Our daughter, Jeannette, celebrated her second birthday on December 1, 1982, one of the hottest days on record for that date: 78 degrees. I sat on the curb under the blazing sun as cars sped by. Why on a curb? I had run over some sharp objects, which resulted in *two* flat tires. Of course, I had only one spare, but not one spare dime to buy a second tire.

I broke down. I was incredibly frustrated—with Mom, with the failing business, with myself because I couldn't seem to make anything work right. I just wanted to give up everything and disappear. Nothing seemed to be going my way. These two flat tires became my tipping point.

"I need you, Lord, now more than ever." It was a simple prayer, but it held all my desperation.

I had to get a job in a hurry in order to support the family. Sue had worked in the deli right up to the day before Jeannette was born. She rested less than a couple of weeks and was back to work. My mom insisted on working at the deli too, which was burdensome rather than helpful, but we couldn't decline her demand that we hire her. I had landed a job as a loan officer trainee with Allied Bank of Texas. Although I already had experience in Canada, I was in a different country, so I had to start at the bottom.

But on that fateful day in December, I reached the end of my rope—just where God wanted me.

Chapter Sixteen

——•——

MAHASHABA

WHEN SUE AND I MOVED TO HOUSTON in September 1980, I was thirty years old and already had five years of lending experience from having worked as a branch manager for Household Finance Company in Toronto. So when I interviewed with a Houston bank for a loan officer trainee job, I was confident that not only would I get the job but also that I would be promoted in no time. I was already familiar with most of the procedures, so it was a no-brainer that I would quickly move up the ranks.

Don Anderson, Senior Vice President, hired only two guys out of over twenty applicants. He told me and the other new guy, Richard, that we were in a competition. A promotion would be available in a short time. Anderson would pick the better one of us to fill the spot.

I took one look at Richard and chuckled to myself. I

had no worries. He looked like a country bumpkin just off the bus from Nowheresville. I pictured myself, with my years of experience over this newbie, already at the finish line of this little competition.

Within just a couple of months, Mr. Anderson called for a staff meeting, where he would announce the "winner" and recipient of the promotion. I fairly strutted into the room. Mentally, I was already patting myself on the back and planning a dinner out with Sue, celebrating my financial prowess.

Mr. Anderson stood smiling at the head of the table. "I know you've all been waiting to hear who I'll be promoting."

I straightened my tie and pushed back my chair, preparing to stand to accept my colleagues' congratulations.

"Richard, you've been an outstanding loan officer trainee. Welcome to your new position!"

A smattering of applause shattered my hope. Richard got the promotion? It made no sense. I knew far more than he did. I felt insulted and humiliated. I held my emotions in check as I trudged back to my cubicle. But I could not control my anger as I drove home.

As I shared the bad news with Sue, I couldn't hold back my tears of shame and deep disappointment. Sue encouraged me not to give up on my job. "There will be other opportunities for promotions. Not getting this one isn't the end of the world. Besides, trust in God, not your job. He's not finished with you yet."

Of course, she was right. And I couldn't quit. We needed the income. The deli was making barely enough to cover the overhead. So although I was discouraged, I continued to do my best at work, always with an eye on the next available promotion.

Don Anderson hired another young recruit, George Hicks, fresh out of the University of Texas. George's father was the CEO of a different local bank and obviously wanted to groom his son to take his place. Mr. Anderson told me to teach this kid while I waited for the next loan officer's job to open up. George was smart and quick to learn; it was a joy training him.

Within a few months, a loan officer position came available. Once again, Mr. Anderson assembled us for a staff meeting to announce who would get the promotion.

Of course, I felt certain I would receive the promotion. After all, Anderson had alluded to that when he told me to train George. Though I wasn't as cocky as I'd been at Richard's promotion, I fully expected my name to be announced. But I remained calm and dignified.

Standing at his place at the head of the table in the conference room, Mr. Anderson acted as if he was announcing the lottery winner. In his Texas drawl, he said, "I am happy to announce that George Hicks has been promoted to loan officer."

I felt like a bomb had exploded, destroying my hopes and dreams—again. I could not believe my ears.

How could this be? I thought the world was turning upside down. My thoughts were, *This pure injustice cannot be allowed. I must sue. I must find a lawyer, but first I must quit, because I can't take this discriminatory humiliation anymore. This is ridiculous to the point of insanity.*

It's a miracle that I arrived home that night in one piece. As I drove, I had to keep wiping tears from my eyes so I could see the road. My emotions were a mixture of rage and sadness. I had thoughts of revenge and even suicide.

After dinner, I went outside our ground-floor apartment and, in the quiet of Houston's muggy summer night, raised my fist toward the starry sky and fumed. "If you, God, are real, why are you letting this unspeakable injustice go on? What is the logic behind this, other than to simply make me miserable?"

I thought of Jeannette, our precious gift from God. Had it not been for her, I would have quit my job, regardless that we had no savings. But she counted on me to provide for her, so walking away from my job or life was not an option. I was in a terrible situation, and I had no choice in the matter. I felt sorry for myself.

Sue was my comforter and my voice of wisdom. She warned me against giving up on God. He had not deserted me, she said, but by my attitude, I was accepting defeat and not trusting God with my life.

That's when she showed me the verse from Jeremiah 29:11: "'For I know the plans I have for you,' declares the LORD, 'plans to prosper you and not to harm you, plans to give you hope and a future.'"

Her words soothed and brought healing to my broken spirit, and God's Word brought life to my injured soul. God had a plan for my life, one filled with hope and a future He'd personally designed. I was going through only one small segment of life, but if I would continue to put my trust in this promise from Jeremiah and not be dismayed, God would bring this plan together so I could live the good life He had conceived for me.

Mahashaba is the Hebrew word meaning "blueprint." It's the Hebrew word that is translated "plans" in Jeremiah 29:11. Let's substitute "plan" with "blueprint": God has the *blueprint* for my life. The *blueprint* is not to harm me, but to prosper me and to give me hope and a future.

Just as an architect considers the purpose of a building as well as its structural integrity, he or she designs it to look good, to function well, and to endure. God does this and more with our lives.

I had been walking around in defeat. You could see it on my expression; it was evident in the slump of my shoulders. Sue encouraged me to walk with the conviction of this word. Her candor was painful, but she was spot on. I had to hear it. I got down on my knees next to my bed and shed tears of remorse and desperation. I asked the Lord for forgiveness and courage to face the situation head on.

So I intentionally began to live with Jeremiah 29:11 in my mind and heart. Every time I sensed colleagues watching me, I said this verse to myself. When out of the corner of my eye I caught someone observing me, I recited the verse silently. I must have repeated it thousands of times until the word became so enmeshed in my thinking and doing that it fused with my DNA. I began to understand that my life was like a book, and the present was simply a page, not the end. I learned to accept whatever came my way, believing God would use every situation to carry out the blueprint of my life. Peace and confidence in the Lord became a natural way of living.

I grabbed hold of this truth so that it no longer mattered where I was or where I was headed. All that mattered was that God had a good plan for me, and I would trust Him with my life.

Chapter Seventeen

—◆—

RESTORATION

Don Anderson called for another staff meeting for an important announcement. By then I had low expectations of receiving a promotion, yet peace reigned in my heart. I would walk in God's blueprint for my life. Period.

But the meeting wasn't about promotions. Mr. Anderson announced that he was leaving and moving to another bank. Frank Mendoza would take his position. Frank, a quiet and able worker, was one of the bank's vice presidents. One of the first things he did in his new position was to call me into his office.

"Robert, I want you to know that I appreciate your devotion to your work despite all the difficulty Anderson put you through. So effective today, I am promoting you to the loan desk."

I learned that Frank was a committed Christian and had noticed the difference in me. He concluded that I must be a Christian also.

So I moved into a new office and eagerly started my new position. It was a joyous occasion, and I felt I was finally vindicated. I received a substantial increase in my salary, but it seemed the raise triggered something hidden deep within me.

Although I was progressing in my walk with the Lord, I didn't recognize the seed of greed that had rooted in my heart. I had repented of many things but never the strong desire for money. I believed money would buy what I didn't have: financial freedom, a house, and a better car for Sue. And then I could give more to the church and missions.

I wined and dined with clients who had deep pockets. Rubbing shoulders with the wealthy allowed me to see the material possessions that could be mine. It was not a spiritually healthy environment for me, given my deep-seated, albeit unperceived, greed. But God, faithful and true, used a particular situation to bring me face to face with my sin so I could rip out greed by the root and place it on the altar of sacrifice once and for all.

One of the clients I wooed to the bank was Jim Hansen. He was married to a cute blonde and lived in the affluent part of Houston. We became such close friends that the line between personal and business relationships blurred.

Jim was an oil broker and lived a high-roller's life. At the time, Houston was booming in oil business. One day, he proposed a deal in which I could make a substantial amount of money in a matter of a few days by buying and selling several hundred barrels of oil. He was cutting a deal with Mike White, an oilman from Vidor, Texas. My part was simply to watch for Jim's $100,000 check to White, payment for the oil, and float it for a few days, giving us enough time to turn around and sell the oil and deposit the proceeds from the sale. Jim had already arranged the sale with another buyer, so once he closed the deal with that guy, he would wire the money from the sale, $150,000, into his account, and then I could release the funds from Jim's account. We would each walk away with a quick profit of $25,000.

It sounded like a solid deal. But as the saying goes, if it seems too good to be true, it probably is. Sadly, but much wiser, I can tell you this saying is true.

Jim and I drove to Hobby Airport to meet White, who had flown in on his private jet. He was the epitome of a cowboy with his Stetson, cowboy boots, and a thick Southern drawl. In the lobby, Jim and White signed the contract, and Jim handed White a check for $100,000. White wanted to verify that the account held sufficient funds, so I called the bank and authorized the payment with the lobby services manager. Satisfied, White promised the oil, shook hands with us, and flew off.

The following day we sent the trucks to pick up the oil, but White was nowhere to be found. I quickly checked the bank account. He had already cashed the check in person. We'd been conned!

I could not see straight. I thought I would pass out. All of sudden my world came crashing down. I realized how quickly I had fallen into temptation and forgotten all the blessings I'd received from the Lord. How ungrateful I was and how aloof I'd become. I saw my greed and it shocked me. Only greed could have driven me to risk my career.

I had brought all this onto myself. I deserved to be fired. My career would go up in smoke, and with this shady transaction on my record, I would never find a job with another bank.

I'd never felt such a depth of sorrow as I did then. And not just because I could be in a lot of trouble, but because I had once again become a failure—to God, to Sue, and even to Frank, who had put so much trust in me. I was truly sorry and repentant. I would face the consequences.

It would be only a matter of days before upper management would question me about how and why I had approved such a transaction, which was clearly outside my authority and strictly against bank policy.

Rather than go to Frank and tell him what I'd

done, I chose to wait out the inevitable. I kept Sue in the dark. I'm sure she could tell by my pensive and subdued attitude that something was up, but she never asked me. During that time I worried, hoped, and, of course, prayed.

I went to work each day and did my job. Several days passed without a word. Coinciding with my foolhardy blunder, upper management was reorganizing. Yet this could not be the reason something of this magnitude had been overlooked. This amount of money would not have passed without someone approving the charge-off. At least the auditors should have caught it.

To this date I do not know what happened, nor can I suggest any plausible theories. All I know is that this event never came up for discussion. It's as if it never happened. It just vaporized somehow. Could it be that God forgave me of my sins and absolved me of the consequences? It's a lesson learned that I've never forgotten. I am a firm believer that nothing happens by chance for those who trust God.

Chapter Eighteen

------ • ------

MARKETER

I CONTINUED TO WORK AT THE BANK. I had a new perspective on my responsibilities, and I focused on giving my best for my employer. My supervisor recognized that my marketing ability was greater than my analytical skills. He encouraged me to apply this skill in my job.

The most important aspect of banking is to earn the clients' trust, especially the wealthy clients. I began building relationships with several law and CPA firms, which led to connections with their partners and leads to individuals.

One day a man walked up to my desk and wanted to open an account. I directed him to the New Account desk, but he seemed irritated. "I was at the bank across the street, but they gave me the runaround. I think they turned me away because of my skin color. I am a Mexican Jew, but the way they treated me, they must not want my million-dollar account."

Okay, I admit it. He had me at "my million-dollar account." I asked him to sit down so we could talk. I learned that he was the owner of the largest chain of hardware stores in Mexico. He'd flown to Houston to open an account. Needless to say, I set up an account with him. That million dollars was just the initial deposit. He brought many more millions after that and introduced me to other millionaires.

I was bringing in millions of dollars in deposits for the bank, which the president quickly noticed in the weekly officers' meetings. I was on a fast track in my banking career. I advanced to a higher position than Richard and George, the other two men who had been promoted before me.

That showed me another facet of God's blueprint for my life. It doesn't matter what people do, God's plan will not be thwarted. He uses every opportunity, good and bad, to accomplish His will. Back when Richard and George had received the promotions I thought were rightfully mine, I boo-hooed, whined, and wailed about it. I gave myself a grand pity party. But looking back at that time, I felt a twinge of shame that I had thrown such a tantrum when God had it all worked out—for my good. It reaffirmed that no matter what situations cross my path, my one task is to trust God and keep following Him. He's got it all under control.

Because of my marketing activities, I met a lot of influential people. God tapped into this to allow me to help others, totally unrelated to the bank. One incident that happened in 1985 some might say was a coincidence. I reject that. It was God working His plan.

John Kim had been attending our church for about a year. I felt compassion for him every time he rolled his wheelchair into the sanctuary. He was a faithful member who never missed the early morning prayers. On this particular day, the education minister called me into his office and asked me if I could help John find a good lawyer for his legal suit against Amoco Oil.

About two years before, John had been working on an oil tanker. In a frantic effort to anchor the ship in Texas City harbor as a severe storm was approaching, he got tangled in the winch he was operating. This accident took a leg and an arm. His loss of blood was so severe it was a miracle he survived. As he was being transported via helicopter to the UTMB emergency center in Galveston, he experienced a personal encounter with Jesus Christ, who told him that his time was not yet up. He had not known who Jesus was until then. This encounter totally transformed his life as he set his heart to pursue Him.

He was a big guy for a Korean, standing over six feet, well-built and muscular from the various martial arts he had mastered. He had also served in the

Special Forces in the Korean Army and had been sent to North Korea.

I told the education minister that I did not have time to help him because of the demands at work, but I would take John to his lawyer once, just to translate for him.

John's lawyer, Eisenberg, was a well-dressed man. His office included a wall of wooden bookshelves filled with various legal tomes. All in all, he presented himself as courteous, intelligent, and professional.

He sat behind his desk, and John and I sat across from him. He explained that there were some "holes" in John's suit because it seemed he hadn't followed the company's protocol during the action that caused his injuries. Eisenberg gave his opinion that Amoco's settlement offer of $2000 per month for his children until they graduated from college, or one lump sum of $150,000, was reasonable.

When I translated this, John's eyes welled up and tears spilled down his cheeks. He said barely above a whisper, "I have been praying for at least a million dollars because I have been dreaming about several different projects and ministries, but now, all those dreams are gone, I guess."

As I dropped him off at his apartment, my heart went out to him. I felt sorry that I could not help him more.

The next day, one of my attorney clients came to my office and asked for an immediate credit on a settlement check he'd received. Normally it takes five days for the check to clear unless the person has an account with a compensating balance. But this guy was a struggling personal injury attorney, often working for other attorneys just to get by. Since I liked the guy, I asked him if he had time to chat with me about another matter.

"Doug, what would be the customary settlement for someone who lost an arm and a leg due to a workplace accident?"

"Of course, depending on the case, the general rule is a million dollars for each limb. Why, do you have someone you want to refer to me?"

As I began explaining John's case to him, he interrupted and said that he was aware of it. That amazed me. Houston had hundreds of attorneys. What was the probability of this one knowing about John's case?

"Why do you suppose Eisenberg had only a $150,000 offer?" I said.

Doug shifted in his seat. He didn't answer right away but crossed and uncrossed his legs.

"What is it, Doug? I get the sense you know something."

He cleared his throat. "Well, I just don't feel

comfortable sharing someone else's case with you."

I badgered him until he finally cracked. "I was working another case for Eisenberg when I learned about the settlement offer."

Amoco had apparently found out that Eisenberg had solicited this case through a broker who had visited John in the hospital. The broker had bribed the ship's captain to accompany him in persuading John to give the case to Eisenberg. Amoco's offer would net him $60,000—40 percent of the settlement. Not a small amount. But he was about to lose the case and run the risk of losing his license to practice law because lawyers are banned from soliciting victims while they are still in recovery. Amoco had learned of the solicitation and threatened to report Eisenberg to the Law Board and have his license revoked.

I immediately called my friend Tim Smith, an attorney, and asked what John should do. He advised that I take John to see Eisenberg. John should then fire him and demand that all documents and materials the lawyer had accumulated be turned over to him immediately.

And that's exactly what we did. I was surprised but thrilled that Eisenberg cooperated. He never asked John why or even tried to talk him out of firing him.

I then set up an appointment with one of the best-known personal injury firms in Houston. When John and I met with the partners of the firm, I found it interesting that they weren't as focused on the details of the accident or the case as much as they were on how the jurors would perceive John. They commented that his physical condition and wheelchair would help elicit compassion and help him solidify his case during the trial.

On the way home from the meeting, both John and I felt good about justice finally coming into play.

The following day, I received a call from one of the partners in the law firm that was representing Amoco. His office was located on the fourteenth floor of my bank building. He wanted to meet with John and me the next day.

As John and I settled in the lawyer's office, he wasted no time with niceties but shot a straight question: "What would be the absolute minimum cash you are willing to settle for without getting any attorneys involved? I mean right now, today."

I translated the question to John. He said he would have settled for $500,000 with a lawyer. So without one, he was willing to settle for $250,000.

Before I translated his answer, I spoke to John in Korean, suggesting that he start at a million dollars and negotiate down from there.

I didn't wait for him to respond before I spoke to the lawyer. "John will settle for one million dollars in cash, but the offer is good only today. If not, we are signing with a top personal injury firm tomorrow." I named the firm.

We left the office, having reached no agreement. The lawyer said only that he would consult with his client.

I hoped I hadn't made matters worse for John by inserting myself into the negotiations as I did.

That evening, I received a call from a representative of Amoco in their Chicago head office. They would agree to the deal, with one condition: John's wife would have to consent to the agreement.

This presented a slight difficulty because she lived in Korea.

John was allowed to stay in the United States only because of the pending lawsuit. He was afraid that once he left the States, he might not be allowed back into the country. Second, he wasn't sure his wife would agree to the deal because of their strained relationship. He pleaded with me to fly to Korea and persuade his wife to sign off on the deal.

That was a tall order. First, I'd have to take time off work, which would be difficult to arrange, and second, I had no idea if I could convince his wife to do this.

Well, I'd gone this far with helping John, and I didn't feel I could walk away. So the next day, I explained the situation to my boss. Surprisingly, he encouraged me to go and even offered to pay my expenses. He figured that if I could make this deal happen, John would deposit his million-dollar settlement into my bank.

I was both nervous and excited to return to Korea. It had been eighteen years since I'd left my country in 1967. At that time I never wanted to return—except to see my family. I had harbored a heart full of bitterness toward Korea and her people because of the treatment I had received.

But the man who was returning to his homeland was not the boy who'd left. I was a Christian, and my perspective of life had changed. I had forgiven those who'd hurt me and released the hurts to the only One who can heal a damaged heart like mine.

As the plane flew over the ocean toward Seoul, my thoughts turned to Korea, and memories of my life there flooded my mind. By the time we landed, I could honestly admit that I missed my country of birth. I longed to be there to renew my acquaintance with her.

I became curious about everything I saw and didn't want to miss seeing everything that flew by as I rode in a taxi to my hotel. The country had gone through a total transformation. I recognized some of the places where I'd spent time with my friends, but most of the streets and buildings had changed beyond recognition, which made me a little sad.

On the other hand, the poverty that was so common while I grew up there seemed to have vanished. In its place were signs of economic progress and affluence. I was proud that my country had made such strides in development.

One of my highlights was a reunion with my best buddies from high school. They were all successful in their careers. But even better than that, they were genuinely happy to see me! Gone were the snide remarks about my mixed race. They had no desire to bully or disparage me. They enjoyed being with me. The only time they made a little fun of me and refused to take me seriously was when I talked about being a Christian and gently tried to tell them about Jesus. Of course, their mocking saddened me, because I know the change Christ could bring to their lives. I hope I at least planted some seeds.

As I later thought about it, these guys had rejected the Savior. I felt I had gained some insight, just a tiny speck, into how Jesus felt when His countrymen rejected Him as their Messiah. I prayed that my buddies, who now fully accepted me as their "brother," would one day accept Jesus as their Savior.

I located John's wife. Contrary to my fear that I would have to plead and coerce her into signing the papers, she put up no fight or argument or anything close to that. In fact, she was very hospitable and even tried to entertain me by buying gifts for my wife and daughter. We met with an attorney from the Seoul law firm Amoco had selected, who took John's wife and me to the US Embassy to have the agreement notarized. I thank God that my task was not burdensome.

When I returned to Houston, Amoco immediately issued a check for a million dollars, which John deposited in my bank.

I lost track of John for several years until I ran into him at a revival meeting in southern Korea. He had divorced his first wife. He had remarried and was attending the revival with his new wife. We found a quiet corner to visit and catch up. When I asked him how he was doing, I was surprised to hear what had happened since we'd last seen each other.

He had returned to Korea, and for a while, he did well. He became popular and went around the country giving testimonies in churches. But the settlement money had made him proud and powerful and subsequently ruined his life. He confessed that he had blown away all his million dollars by gambling and investing in scams. But in the end, he was grateful that God had humbled him. Now he and his wife were truly serving the Lord, with hearts full of love for Him.

Chapter Nineteen

———•———

FAST TRACK

I RETURNED HOME AND CONTINUED TO do well in my job at the bank. My supervisors recognized my ability to attract big money and promoted me on the fast track. I came to understand that although I could woo new customers to my bank, it was God who gave me this ability. I attributed all my blessings to Him. Having this attitude freed me from a lot of pressure. I didn't feel I had to pound the pavement, getting every person who had a six- or seven-figure income to put their money in my bank. Rather, I committed my job to the Lord and worked as though He were my boss.

I also got more involved in the church work and took an immense interest in studying the Bible. Soon the church leadership acknowledged my talent in teaching and management and asked me to run the Sunday school department. Too many Sunday school superintendents accept the job because "somebody's got to do it," and their task becomes a burden because they are not gifted for this work. But for me, stepping into the role of Sunday school superintendent was a joy, not a burden. It was the right job at the right time.

Even my weekday evenings filled up. I had joined the three-year discipleship training taught by our pastor on Tuesdays and attended the Wednesday night service, as well as the Saturday morning prayer gatherings.

I particularly enjoyed working with second-generation Korean teenagers as they strove to find their place between their American and Korean cultures. Because I understood their struggles firsthand, my heart went out to these teens. I invested my time, energy, and money into them and felt good about the results. Most of them attended my class because their parents pressured them into it. However, many of them were leading double lives: studious and submissive in their Korean homes, but rebellious and 100 percent American in school. These kids had real problems, and they trusted me enough to share them and seek my counsel. They began bringing friends involved with gangs, leading dangerous and violent lives. Many of the kids' lives were genuinely transformed, and they became born-again, Spirit-filled, committed Christians.

In 1982, I formed a group called Teen Mission and trained about twenty teenagers in preparation for a tour through several states and Canada. I employed professional dancers, actors, and musicians to train our members so we could minister to thousands using our production, which included dances and a pantomime musical. The group evolved into a year-round ministry. I had to limit the enrollment to forty by putting them through a selection process. Year after year we traveled to additional countries, including South Korea, Japan, and Honduras.

In 1990, after eight years of successfully bringing kids to Christ and training them as ambassadors for their Lord, I turned the ministry over to the education minister of the church and retired from that work. Unfortunately, Teen Mission fizzled out in less than two years. Even so, today the majority of the kids I worked with are successfully serving the Lord through their vocations. Many are pastors, missionaries, doctors, lawyers, and businessmen working in different ministries around the world.

I'll never forget one of the kids, David Dominguez Jr. His father is Mexican American and his mother Korean. David traveled with us for two years while in high school. In our performances, he played the role of a gangster, mainly because he was muscular and had a black belt in Taekwondo. His martial arts movements never failed to impress the audience and were effective in touching the young and old with the message of the gospel. David did well in school also, so well that Rice University offered him a scholarship. Eventually, he went on to Harvard Medical School and became a pediatrician because of his love for kids. He married a strong Christian woman who practices law. They have a beautiful baby daughter. In 2013 he sensed a call from the Lord and took his family and a group of missionaries to Myanmar.

The Lord was working in my heart, too. At first, when my faith was immature, I assumed God was blessing me at work and in finances because I was faithfully attending church and doing church work. But as I grew more in the Lord, I became thirsty for more of God. I believe that God, like any father, loves to give his children most of the things they want, even though He may not approve of them all . . . like a father occasionally gives candy to his child even though he knows sugar isn't healthy and can cause tooth decay. As the child grows, the father expects the child to demand fewer things and to desire to become more like the father. This is how it is with God also.

When I was vice president of a suburban bank, I passed by M Bank on my way to work every morning. I had heard a lot of good things about the institution, and my desire grew to work for them. So I did what any good Christian would do: find a verse that applied to my situation. This is what my pastor taught, as well as many of the evangelists he invited to our church: "Stretch your hand to me and cry out . . ."

So on the way to work in the mornings, I held my right hand stretched toward that bank. "Father, please let me work at this bank." On the way home I stretched out my left hand. "Father, please let me work at this bank."

I had done this for about three months when the president of M Bank called. "Mr. Park, I've heard good things about you. I'd like to get with you and talk business. Can we meet for lunch?"

Long story short: He offered me the position of senior vice president, which included a substantial pay increase. Of course I accepted the offer. And then not long after that, I was promoted to president of a small bank . . . and later to a much larger bank. My experience validated my "I want it, so, God, please give it to me" thinking and belief system.

But as I dug more into the Word, I began to desire blessings of a different kind. I wanted to know my Father in heaven more and to love Him more deeply and intimately. I pursued His spiritual gifts. I was jealous of those few who had visions of Christ or the ability to converse with God. I envied those who claimed to know God's will and to be able to interpret when someone spoke in tongues. Since I had none of these gifts, I felt left out and less blessed. It didn't matter how high I advanced in the bank or how much money I had. I wanted to experience the higher level of His blessings. So I tried fasting and praying for days on end. I attended meetings where the Holy Spirit was supposedly at work. I tuned my ears to the rumors in the Christian communities for any fresh leads of where I might find these abilities.

One time, as I was praying with hundreds of people, I did see Jesus on the cross. He was in pain and bleeding. I stood at his side. He looked down on me, sorrow filling his eyes. I longed for Him to say something to me. Though He never uttered a word, His expression spoke volumes. In an instant, the unspoken message in His eyes implanted itself in my heart and mind: "I am doing this for you because I love you and want to save you. It is unbearable, but I bear it for you. Always remember this: tell others about it and follow Me for the rest of your life."

I burst into tears. As I sobbed and wailed, I would not be consoled. Coming face to face with the horrific suffering and shame my sins had put my Lord through evoked a sorrow I didn't know resided in me. I was at a loss as to how to respond, yet in my own way I suffered with Him. And then I was speaking in some language or sound I had never learned. I was sobbing and rambling at the same time, but it felt good, and I didn't want it to stop. Later I learned it was the gift of tongues.

Then the vision disappeared. I was sad, but at the same time I felt the Lord's favor by allowing this special blessing of seeing Him. It also confirmed that the Lord answered my prayers in a personal way.

Another time, I went to a revival meeting at a small church. I sat in the last row because I had arrived late. At the end of the message, the traveling evangelist said he had a message for someone present but was not getting it clearly. So he prayed more and then pointed his finger at me. "Stand to receive a revelation from the Lord."

Although I was skeptical, I stood.

"I see you like Peter in Acts ten, witnessing heaven opening and a large sheet being let down to earth by its four corners. It contained all kinds of four-footed animals, reptiles, and birds. Peter was told to eat them, but he refused because he regarded them impure and unclean. God wants to bring you out of your own people and send you to the people and nations you have never known or been to."

A strange force penetrated my heart at this point. It was as if this evangelist and I were the only two people in the room. His words awakened something within me. But he wasn't done with his "message."

"God will use you as His mouthpiece, and you shall proclaim His name throughout the world. My son, I have called you out of the country of your birth so that you will serve Me in My kingdom. I have a plan for your life, and the plan is not to harm you but to give you hope and prosperity."

How could this stranger know all this about me? How could he have quoted Jeremiah 29:11, my life verse? Could he have made up this stuff? His words contained too many specifics of my life. I couldn't possibly attribute this to coincidence. Someone had to have revealed this to him—either the Holy Spirit or the Devil himself.

In my pursuit of a deeper walk and knowledge of the Lord, I experienced many more such incidents, too numerous to list them all here. But one day a thought occurred to me, which prompted me to ask God, "Why don't You speak to me directly rather than through a third party?"

I spent much time in prayer and the Word. Though I didn't get an answer with spoken words, I began to mature in the Lord.

Chapter Twenty

———•———

DEATH

IN 1988 I FOUND OUT THROUGH A MUTUAL friend that Chuck Lee, my Amerasian buddy from Seoul and housemate at Ms. Buck's Hilltop house, was living in Portland, Oregon. I was excited to find him, since we had lost track of each other after the blowup with Ted Harris and the Foundation. The last time we'd seen each other was just before he shipped out to Vietnam in 1970.

I contacted him. "Hey, Chuck, I'd really like to see you."

"I'll be in Tacoma, Washington, for business. I'm selling real estate. Any chance you can meet me there?"

I took some time off work and flew to Portland, Oregon. From there I rented a car and drove along the beautiful, rugged northern Pacific coast to Tacoma. I was looking forward to our reunion, to catch up with each other and fill in the years we'd been apart. I was pumped!

My heart sank when we hooked up. Where and the condition I found him was disheartening. He had been spending several days at his friend's one-room, sparsely furnished apartment. Empty beer and liquor bottles lay strewn on the counter and tables. Even in our days in Philadelphia, his heavy drinking had concerned me. But this sight convinced me he'd become a full-blown alcoholic.

We began talking about what had occurred during the years we'd been apart. He said that after the tour in Vietnam, he was assigned to Korea, where he met and married an Amerasian girl. They had two daughters but were now divorced.

"She ruined my life. She ran off with some man she met in the factory."

His hatred consumed him. He continued his profanity-filled diatribe, in which he called both his wife and her boyfriend the most vulgar names imaginable. I could almost see venom spewing out with each complaint. But rather than being offended by his foul accusations and make a hasty exit, I felt compassion for my friend. What a rough life he had lived!

Since he didn't have a car, I drove him wherever he wanted to go. We went to Seattle and met a group of Amerasians who seemed to have adjusted well in their fatherland. In fact, many of them were outgoing and friendly. Most were subcontractors providing janitorial services for the airlines and airport buildings at SeaTac. I enjoyed meeting these people and getting to know some of Chuck's friends.

Since Chuck had completed his business in Tacoma, we drove back to Portland together. The two-hour drive afforded me the opportunity to have a heart-to-heart talk with him. I began by sharing my life in Canada, how I'd struggled to find the answers to my questions about my purpose in life, about death and the possibility of an afterlife. I told him how I had searched to find something permanent and eternal.

After a few sips of beer, he started to open up about his many life-threatening experiences in Vietnam. I could relate to this, so I told him about the incident of the mine explosion in Sudbury, Ontario. Then I presented the gospel and the need to forgive his ex-wife. But I also told him that for his own well-being he'd have to forgive others, too: the Koreans who cursed him, Pearl Buck, Ted Harris, and those who had hurt him. "You may think you've got a lot of people against you, but I can tell you this with full assurance, Jesus is *for* you. He is on your side, and He will never betray you, disappoint you, or abandon you."

I repeated this several times. I knew my words were touching a tender place, because tears welled in his eyes. He quickly swiped them away and worked to compose himself. This was the Chuck I knew—the guy who believed he had to always be tough.

"Would you consider inviting this Jesus into your life?"

Chuck paused a moment. "Let me think about it."

I didn't want to press him any further. His decision had to be his own, from the prompting of the Holy Spirit, not because he felt pressure from me.

We stopped at a nice restaurant for dinner and talked some more. It felt good to reconnect. I dropped him off near his apartment. My heart broke when I waved before I pulled away. He looked like the loneliest soul on this earth. I determined to stay in touch and not lose contact again. My heart ached for him as I flew back to Houston.

A few months later, I received a call telling me that Chuck had died in a swimming accident in the Pacific Ocean. He had been invited to someone's birthday party. He got drunk, dove into the icy ocean water, and died of a heart attack.

I was shocked and devastated. After leaving Chuck in Portland, I had continued to pray for him to find peace in Jesus. But it appeared nothing had changed in his life. My heart was heavy with this tragic loss of a friend. We'd had similar life experiences, yet the big difference lay in our relationship with God.

Chapter Twenty-One

CANCER

My mother started smoking cigarettes during the war and continued most of her life. She told me that on some days she was so miserable that she would roll up dried squash leaves and light up when she couldn't afford to buy cigarettes.

In 1990 we had been in Houston for ten years. She had not changed her attitude toward Sue and was still demanding and controlling, yet we loved her.

One day we noticed she was coughing constantly. We thought it was a lingering cough from a cold, but after two weeks it had not improved. We became concerned and took her to the doctor, who ordered tests. An X-ray showed a small spot in her lungs. The doctor suggested we take Mom to M.D. Anderson Cancer Center.

I knew Dr. David Seong, who worked as an associate professor there. He kindly provided a way for us to admit Mom right away, and he arranged for her care.

One of the first things the doctors did was a biopsy. Because of her long-term smoking, it was no surprise that she had an aggressive, small-cell lung cancer. She began receiving chemotherapy and radiation treatments, which, of course, made her sick. She began losing weight. She was already a tiny woman, no more than four feet eight inches, and with the weight loss, she looked like a child lying in the big hospital bed.

Sue and I alternated taking time off work to care for Mom at the hospital. Initially, the tumor seemed to have disappeared, and the chief physician gave us hope that she may have fought off the cancer. At this good news, we all seemed to breathe more easily and ventured to make plans for Mom to return home. But Dr. Seong cautioned my optimism by pointing out that the cancer cells may be dormant in the blood stream and could roar back to life.

Roar back it did after about six months. We were offered two options. One was for Mom to undergo major surgery to remove one of her lungs. This was not practical because the chemo and radiation had decimated her body. She weighed only seventy pounds and was as weak as a newborn. Just mentally picturing the surgeon cracking open Mom's rib cage scared me off. The second option was to use an experimental drug for which, at that time, we had no data as to its effectiveness or side effects. We chose the second option.

Mom received several rounds of chemotherapy with this new drug, but the treatment further weakened her with no visible sign of the cancer being affected. Finally, we were told that the doctors and medical science could do nothing more for her. They said we should take her home, make her comfortable, and prepare for her death. The doctor warned me that she would experience much pain, so we would need to administer morphine shots.

I'm sorry to say that I could not bear the sight of her condition. Sue took care of Mom more than I did. She played her guitar and sang hymns and prayed for her every day. Mom's heart began to mellow.

One day she said to Sue, "You know, I have grown to like you. In fact, I love you more than I love my son."

Mom loved to hear the hymn "Out of My Bondage, Sorrow and Night" and often asked Sue to sing it over and over.

"Do you think I can also believe in the same Jesus you do?"

Fighting tears of joy and gratitude, Sue led Mom to receive the Lord as her Savior.

When Sue told me about this, I was delirious with joy. This was the purpose of our moving ten years prior and suffering Mom's difficult behavior toward us. But it was all worth it to usher Mom into the hands of our Lord. God is good! Thank you, Jesus!

You'd think I would have been walking on cloud nine, rejoicing and praising God. Well, I did . . . then I had doubts about Mom's salvation. Did she really understand how and why the Lord came to this earth and died on the cross? Did she realize the weight of her sins and the absolute impossibility of absolving them without the blood of Jesus Christ? I wasn't sure of the answers, but I desperately wanted to believe she was saved. I prayed without ceasing for assurance of her salvation.

Shortly after Sue led Mom to the Lord, Mom was hospitalized for the last time. While I was with her, a couple of ladies from our church visited her to pray for her. By then she was so weak she couldn't respond, even to simple conversations. She slipped in and out of consciousness. Mrs. Yeo and Mrs. Kim had a ministry of visitation, and they were both prayer warriors. If you needed prayer, you wanted these two godly women interceding for you. As they were praying for Mom, I was somewhat surprised they didn't pray for healing but simply lifted up praise after praise.

And then something totally unexpected occurred. My mom started to pray in an unknown language. She spoke several languages—Japanese, Chinese, English, and Korean—but this language wasn't any of them. The two ladies immediately recognized it to be tongues, as they also often spoke in tongues when they prayed. It must have been the work of the Holy Spirit.

This was my assurance of her genuine salvation, that she understood her need for a Savior. A tremendous sense of peace and relief washed over my entire being. As tears streamed down my cheeks, my joy was complete. I took it as a sure sign from the Lord, who cared about my concern so much that giving my mom this gift was His way of answering my prayers. Don't get me wrong, I am not saying that speaking in tongues validates one's salvation, for that is not in line with biblical teaching. However, I am simply stating how I felt . . . or rather how the Lord made me feel under those circumstances.

When the doctors told us they could do nothing for Mom, we brought her home, knowing she would soon depart for her permanent home with Jesus in heaven. Only a short time after we got Mom settled, my half sister, Yuni, barged into my room at about 2:00 one morning, frantically waking me up. As we raced to Mom's room, Yuni said that Mom had been breathing with difficulty and then stopped breathing altogether. Out of desperation, I administered mouth-to-mouth resuscitation, but after several minutes there was no response. That was meant to be my good-bye kiss to my mom.

She died in peace and without pain. The doctors marveled that she never needed the morphine shots.

The funeral service was memorable. She had lived through some important chapters of human history. She'd overcome numerous obstacles, but her ultimate victory came to her with eternal life because of the Lord she believed in. Though she accepted the Lord late in life, it was her most important life event.

One of the most poignant moments of the service came when my son, Timothy, who was six at the time, peered into the coffin. Seeing his grandmother's lifeless body, he backed away and shot me a look I'll never forget. His eyes wide, he tipped his head and said, "Dad, didn't you say she's gone to heaven?"

"Yes, Son, she sure has."

"Then how come she's still here?"

I had to think about my answer. Naturally, we'd taught my son that when a believer dies, he or she goes to heaven. To a six-year-old's literal way of thinking, that meant body, soul, and spirit transported to heaven. So why was his grandmother's body still there? Isn't childlike faith marvelous?

I was at a loss for words to answer my son in a way he could grasp. Actually, I don't remember what I said to explain it for him, but I probably stumbled my way through it to convince him that the soul and spirit meet with God in heaven, but the body would have to go into the ground and wait for the resurrection.

Whatever I said and however I said it seemed to satisfy my young son's need to understand that the essence of his grandmother that made her who she was—her spirit—was now well and whole and enjoying eternal life with Jesus.

Chapter Twenty-Two

————•————

THE DECISION

I WAS APPROACHING MY FORTIETH BIRTHDAY when I started to reexamine my life, partly because some mature members in my church sensed a call in my life and encouraged me to seek the Lord for clarity. I asked myself several probing questions: Am I going in the direction that I will be content to pursue for the rest of my life? Am I fully tracking God's *mahashaba*, God's blueprint, for my life? Am I missing a call He may have on my life? I didn't want to miss out on any part of God's plan. That would be a tragedy, and all my endeavors would have been in vain.

This evaluation/struggle went on for about a year, until I decided to quit my banking career and enroll in Southwestern Baptist Theological Seminary. I had chosen a path of no return. Naturally, many folks, including some fellow Christians, thought I was nuts. Even my kids assumed my decision meant that we would have to sell my BMW and our house. I didn't think so, but even if it did mean letting go of nice possessions, I could not ignore what Jesus kept ringing in my heart: "No one who puts his hand to the plow and looks back is fit for service in the Kingdom of God" (Luke 9:62).

I knew that choosing this course might cost me dearly, but I was willing. After all, the grace I received did not come cheap—Jesus paid with His own life. But little did I know to what extent I was going to pay. Had I known all the obstacles, suffering, and difficulties waiting for me, I probably would not have eagerly jumped in. Our human fear is one of the great reasons why God does not reveal all that is involved in His plans for our lives.

Although carrying a heavy study load at my age was, shall we say, challenging, it was truly enjoyable and enlightening. I especially relished the interaction with other students who were spiritually mature and earnest.

When I left my job at the bank, Sue and I collected our assets and, along with a bank loan, purchased an office supply-printing company located in downtown Houston. (We had sold the deli earlier.) The income generated from the business would carry me through seminary and provide our living expenses. A small Korean church in Galveston also called me to be their pastor. This was part-time employment and involved driving sixty miles each way, while carrying a full load at the seminary and running the business. Where my studies challenged me mentally, the church and business challenged me physically. I usually slept no more than four hours a day and endured one-hundred-hour work weeks. But this is where God had me, so I did it all with gladness.

Around the same time, God gave me an opportunity to go to Chile and preach the gospel. I was introduced to a missionary who had been working in the prisons. She was well connected to the wife of the Minister of Interior, who issued a special pass so she could enter any prison in that country. Starting with the prison in the northernmost city of Arica and on to Osorno in the south, we visited several dozen prisons and held services with the inmates.

The conditions were inhumane, and my heart broke for the prisoners. All prisons were over-crowded and poorly equipped. What windows were there had no glass, subjecting the inmates to the harsh temperatures of the desert heat up north and the frigid winters down south. The wretched and filthy bathrooms were unfit for animals, much less humans. The inmates did not have adequate food, and hygiene was sorely lacking.

One time I was preaching to about a hundred inmates in Osorno when I saw a blind man coming forward to receive Christ. He had tears rolling down his cheeks as he confessed his sins and welcomed the Lord into his heart. Later he gave his testimony, which I still remember as though it were yesterday.

He had been a member of a gang that robbed banks. After one such heist, his partner betrayed him and another member by shooting them and taking off with the loot. The other robber died. But this man survived, although he lost sight in both eyes. Originally, he had been incarcerated in a different prison, and on the day he went to jail for the bank robbery, he vowed that he would find the partner and kill him. Eventually, he learned that this partner had been sent to the Osorno prison. This blind man requested a transfer to Osorno.

After a long wait, his transfer came through. He finally arrived in Osorno only a month prior to my visiting and preaching. Every day he waited to run into the guy so he could murder him.

Then, at his cellmate's urging, he came to the meeting where I was speaking. My topic had been about what it had cost God to bring forgiveness of our sins so we may be reconciled to Him. The blind man could not resist the call of God. As he made his way to the front with the aid of his cellmate, he broke down in tears and asked for forgiveness of his sins. He also knew he had to forgive his former partner in crime. One more precious soul had been added to the kingdom that day.

Visiting and preaching in these jails was tremendously emotional yet deeply gratifying. As I flew back home, I prayed, giving thanks and telling the Lord that I wanted to do this kind of work for Him for the rest of my life.

I continued to return to Chile and spent my time and energy in preaching and teaching to the point of total exhaustion. But I loved it. I loved fulfilling God's call on my life.

Chapter Twenty-Three

THE CALL

AFTER THREE YEARS OF HARD WORK, IN 1994 I graduated with a Master of Divinity degree, Biblical Languages Concentration. As I prayed for a ministerial position, I assumed God would use me either in an Anglo church or in a Korean church for some kind of English ministry. Then came the first offer: from a Korean church. But they were proposing the position of senior pastor, something I had not contemplated.

I felt honored to be considered for such a position, for I was a fresh seminary graduate. I quickly learned there was a catch to the call. This congregation was the result of a division in the church where Sue and I had previously served for a number of years. And the leader of the group who led that revolt was well-known in the Korean community. His words and actions made it clear to all that he was not a Christian. But it was he who called me and extended the invitation to come and preach on Sunday. At the mention of his name, Sue refused to hear the rest of the offer. "No. Absolutely not. This offer is not even worth deliberating."

Though I agreed that this position wasn't for me, I did not want to appear discourteous by refusing to entertain his offer, so I stalled for time before I planned on turning him down.

In the meantime, I accepted an invitation by Che Ahn to attend one of his conferences in Pasadena, a few miles northeast of Los Angeles. Che was a second-generation Korean pastor who led a fast-growing, multiethnic church in Pasadena. He was hosting a conference and strongly urged me to come. The last time I'd seen Che was about seven years prior when I was working with Teen Mission. Back then I had invited him to lead a revival in English for the second-generation Koreans, as well as others in our church.

I thought it would be good to get away from Houston for a while. A learning and networking opportunity also appealed to me. What I didn't know until I got there was that Che had joined the Vineyard movement. He had invited to this conference some key pastors involved in Vineyard. Honestly, I was somewhat appalled by the disorderly conduct of the people who were supposedly ministering to others while worship was going on. Some people shook and jerked before falling on the floor, slithering and squirming about. I could not see the relevance of this to the Bible or the purpose of the Holy Spirit, whom they claimed was doing this. I watched and listened but with skepticism.

My doubt was challenged when the wife of one of the associate pastors spoke at one of the sessions. She specifically called me out of the crowd to come forward, saying she had a prophecy for me. I had never met her before, and I felt certain that Che could not have had the time to tell her about me. Even if he had, he would not have been able to describe me so that she could have singled me out of a thousand attendees.

She said that she was seeing some kind of manual in a binder, perhaps some sort of training manual. "Ah, yes, it is the discipleship training. You have been praying and thinking about that. God says that He approves of what you are doing. God also has this message for you: 'I am pleased with your love for Me and the genuine spirit you have. I want you to know that I am the One who created you and have laid out the path for you to follow. I am pleased with the way you pursue Me. I will raise you up in due time and use you for My glory. I have chosen you to represent Me to the world. I will send you to faraway places to people you have not known, and you shall teach them about My love for them.

"'I have called you to minister to My people, but

you are hesitating. Why are you trying to go the way of Jonah? I will be with you and help you and give you what you need. Be bold and courageous, for it is I who make the plans and make them possible. My son, I have already determined your future—the future of hope and glory.'"

This message was incredible, since no one, including Sue, knew about what I had been thinking and praying. I had been writing a discipleship manual, which I kept the draft in a binder! No one knew about this either.

Before this woman was finished with the last sentence, something indescribable spread from my heart all the way to the top of my brain. While attending the Baptist seminary, I had developed a solid systematic and orthodox theology, which limited prophecy to the proclamation of the Word and didn't include foretelling future events. In fact, my guard immediately flew up whenever I heard someone spout a foretelling prophecy, because foretelling was limited to the Old Testament and ceased when the writing of the New Testament was complete. Granted, this is a valid caution because I'd seen several "prophets" abuse or conjure this gift for the purpose of financial gain and self-promotion.

But in this encounter, my assumptions and carefully constructed belief about prophecies crumbled. All of a sudden, my knees buckled and I fell on the floor. This woman knelt next to me and continued to offer up prayers for me. They sounded like angels singing.

Later that evening, I called Sue and shared this with her. I'm not sure what I expected her to say, but her reaction—dead silence—was not it. To be honest, I was confused myself. I knew the phrase "but you are hesitating" referred to the call as senior pastor that neither Sue nor I wanted. But to my way of thinking, it was more important that we obeyed God's plan, regardless of our likes or dislikes.

We struggled with the validity of this prophecy and never came to understand why it happened the way it did. But I have come to believe that possibly the most important lesson I learned from this experience is never to limit what God can do. I am to be open to anything or anyone God puts in my path. If He wants to convey His message, He can use a donkey—as He did with Balaam—because He's not limited by time or manmade conventions.

Eventually, Sue and I decided to trust Him, and I reluctantly accepted the invitation to be the senior pastor of this break-off church.

Just as I feared, I walked into a lions' den. The church had two groups bickering about power and control. My pleas and preaching went over their heads. In fact, the more I tried to mitigate the situation, the worse it got. Both factions turned their criticism on me, as I refused to take sides. I spent many sleepless nights over the struggle, and I devoted numerous days to fasting and praying. The only thing I gained was frustration and misery because I saw no improvement in the situation.

In one early morning prayer service on Saturday, I was startled to see a group of men who usually did not attend these meetings sitting in the front row. They represented my opposition. Afterward, during individual prayer time, I heard one of the men whisper, "Why is this Yankee taking so long with his prayer?" In his question, he used an expletive that not only accurately described my parentage but also revealed his immaturity and wrong heart.

As soon as I was done praying, they barged into my office and demanded my resignation, effective immediately.

I was tempted to give in, but an inner voice prevented me from doing that. After all, it was God who had told me to accept this position, and I should wait until He told me to leave. I would not be swayed by men. I refused to give in to their demands. They became irate and threatened further action.

Though I eventually stayed in for a total of five years, which turned out to be the record length of time any pastor had stayed with that congregation, I still had some hard lessons to learn while pastoring this church.

Chapter Twenty-Four

―――•―――

THE STALKER

DURING MY FIRST PASTORATE, A WOMAN named June came to our church at the urging of another member. She seemed insecure and on edge. Yet she rarely missed a service or event in the church. She frequently asked me to pray for her, which I gladly did.

One day she set up an appointment for counseling. When we met, she revealed her past and broke down in uncontrollable sobs.

June had been an aspiring art student in Korea and liked to hang around with *opas* who were artists. *Opa* is a Korean word meaning "older brother," but the term is used by younger girls to refer to their boyfriends who are older. June was pretty, and the *opas* favored her. But one day at a party, she had gotten drunk and passed out. More than a dozen *opas* gang-raped her. She became so ashamed of herself that she left her parents and home and turned to selling her body to American GIs.

During this time she met a nineteen-year-old soldier who was eight years younger than June. Something clicked between them and shortly thereafter they married, and he brought June to the United States. Unfortunately, he was addicted to cocaine, alcohol, and sex, and he involved June in these activities. As time passed, June's husband started to have relationships with other women involved in his same addictions. Eventually he left her and their three-year-old daughter.

As a single mom, she moved to Houston and landed a job at a Japanese restaurant. Dressed in a kimono, she entertained and served Japanese businessmen. She caught the eye of one of her customers, an engineer working for a Japanese firm in Houston. Their relationship grew and deepened, and they ultimately married.

As June told me her story, I was so saddened by her hard life that I nearly broke down myself. I felt I could help her by teaching her to yield to God's healing power. So we set up weekly sessions. She faithfully attended each meeting, and she seemed to make improvements, for which I was thankful.

At this time I was organizing a mission trip to Haiti, where we had been working with a local pastor to show the film *Jesus* in Creole, the language of the Haitians. June joined the dozen or so members who planned to go.

During the trip I noticed unusual behavior in her, which raised a red flag for me. Whenever the group would drive to some place, she manipulated it so that she sat next to me. To make me even more uncomfortable, she would let her legs touch mine, although she acted as though it was unintentional. As much as I began to keep a distance from her, she became even more bold and obvious.

What a dilemma. I didn't want to rebuff her and risk hurting her already-damaged feelings, yet I did not want her throwing herself at me. Neither did I desire to encourage her in any way.

On the day before we were to leave Haiti, all the members wanted to go to the nearby beach one last time. As we were playing around in the water, she approached me in her bikini and stuck close to me— uncomfortably close. I tried to avoid her, but she would not be put off. As our group was heading back to our cabins to get ready for dinner, I waited to leave to make sure everyone was accounted for. June also stayed behind. And then, she asked, "Pastor, is it wrong to think about someone all the time?"

I feared where she was going with this. "That all depends on who that person is."

Then she dropped the bomb. "I think about you all the time; I even dream about you. I try so hard not to, but it's just impossible. I feel such joy when I think about you. I feel so much better about myself."

"June, I do not want to hear this. It's wrong."

Then she tried to kiss me. I pushed her away. She stomped off, crying out loud and embarrassing me. I feared that if our members saw this display, they might misunderstand the situation.

"June, please, you've got to come to your senses and stop acting like this. Go get dressed and join the rest for dinner."

She did as I said and sat with us for dinner, but she refused to eat. Of course, this drew everyone's attention to her. She pouted for the rest of the evening, which made things even more awkward.

I thought my warning her to stop her improper behavior, followed by my brush-off, put an end to her advances. But I was wrong. The next day, while we were at the airport in Port-au-Prince, she made a scene by insisting that the person assigned to the seat next to me change with her. I'm so thankful this person was wise enough not to yield to her demand. In fact, she saw through June's tactic. Not giving up her seat next to me was her way of protecting me. Needless to say, I flew back to Houston with a heavy burden on my heart.

Back home the situation with June worsened. She started calling me and demanding that I meet with her outside the church. She would not take no for an answer.

My life was turning into a scene from a Dean

Koontz psychological thriller. June started following me wherever I went. She waited in her car for hours, clearly hoping to see me come out of the church. She trailed me to my workouts and even to my appointments. It wasn't long before she knew my daily routine.

I knew the risk involved, especially with the embroiled state of my church at the time. If—or when—my opponents were to catch on to June's behavior toward me, they would not hesitate to use it to achieve their goal of booting me out as their pastor. I had jealously guarded two of my strengths so that no one could find fault: my preaching and my ethical standards. I needed desperately to hang on to both. Though I was innocent of any wrongdoing, June's behavior had the power to destroy my reputation.

My frustration reached its peak the day I was in a hurry to visit one of the church members in the hospital. My stomach flip-flopped when I opened the garage door and saw that June had pulled her car into the driveway of my house, blocking my vehicle.

"Please, June, I need you to move your car. I have some visitation I must do. People are waiting for me."

"Let me come with you. We can talk while you drive."

I looked up and down the street, hoping no neighbors were watching. "Look, you've been following me around lately, and it's embarrassing. My children are about to come home from school, and they would think that your being here, hindering me from leaving, is really odd."

But she would not budge, and I eventually gave in. I figured she'd cause a scene if I didn't relent. Well, even though I did relent, she still caused a scene, though not one I had imagined. While we were driving, she started to strip naked in broad daylight. I pulled into a nearby parking lot and demanded that she stop.

"Robert, I'm yours. All of me. We belong together. Riding with you makes me so happy; we should do it more often. And I don't mind waiting for hours while you take care of church business. If we're together, I'm content."

I realize now that she had deeper issues that I was not qualified to deal with. She had constructed a fantasy world in which I was the central figure. June was not rational in her thinking, so trying to reason with her was futile. Irrationality and reason can never meet.

Her stalking me went on almost every day, June manipulating me to do what she wanted by threatening to tell my wife and the church that we'd had a physical relationship in the car. I was horrified and didn't know how to handle this situation. My nerves were stretched tight, and I spent many sleepless nights worrying about what June would do next and if she'd carry out her threat and spread vicious lies. What would Sue think? Would this end my marriage? I hadn't told Sue about June. I truly believed this situation wasn't worth discussing because it would be resolved soon.

But as it protracted, it became more difficult to reveal to Sue because I feared she might not believe me then—after all, the situation was rather bizarre. I kept wishing the problem would just go away so I wouldn't have to tell my wife at all. But it had been going on— and growing—for almost a year. Telling her at this point would raise even more suspicion, since I'd harbored this secret for so long.

How would the church members react? How could I explain the situation, if at all? Many pastors had lost their careers because of false accusations. And what about my children, who were then old enough to form their own opinions?

I was most miserable because I was not able to minister to the people the way I had always done before. I felt like a hypocrite, and I had a hard time praying earnestly either in private or in public. Although I knew many pastors, I didn't feel I could confide in them.

One evening, June called my wife and said her life was a mess. Sue thought June was having marital problems. She suggested that June and her husband meet with us to discuss the matter. June asked if she could come to our house. To my horror, Sue readily agreed.

June arrived alone. Her puffy, red-rimmed eyes

indicated she'd been crying. As Sue tried to talk to her, June wept and babbled about things that made no sense. She said she hated herself and wanted to end her life. She went on and on about feeling misunderstood by others, even those in the church, and how miserable she was living with her current husband. Then she sobbed that God must hate her and that she was so unfortunate. She just went all over the map with her ranting. Sue feared June might be suicidal.

Just when I thought things couldn't get worse, June asked if she could sleep at our house that night. Sue agreed to let her sleep in our guest room.

After an alarmingly short period of time, June had gone from standing too close to me to claiming her space in my house. My nightmare was coming to life before my eyes.

But it was about to escalate.

Chapter Twenty-Five

————•————

THE SPLIT

JUNE TOLD SOME LADIES IN THE CHURCH that she'd had an intimate relationship with me. Naturally, the lie spread like the Black Death. Church members took sides and rapidly became polarized. My nightmare that June would irreparably damage my ministry and marriage began to unfold.

When I stood up to her, she unleashed her venom.

The trigger that ignited this lie occurred when I was driving home after the Wednesday evening service. I saw through the rearview mirror that June was trailing me again. Anger got the best of me, so I decided to shake her off. I drove like a racecar driver, changing lanes erratically and speeding up to 100 miles an hour on Interstate 10. Honestly, I even hoped she would get into a terrible accident while trying to keep up with me. But, to my surprise and chagrin, she was not only able to keep up with me but also safely. As I neared the entrance to my subdivision, I feared she would follow me all the way into the house.

I pulled over and jumped out of my car. Not giving her the chance to get into my car, I went back to hers and got in. I could see she was becoming seriously unhinged, yet in my ignorance of her mental condition, I still thought I could reason with her.

Tears streamed down her face. She was emotional, agitated, and angry that I had tried to run away from her. Before I could say a word, the unthinkable happened. She pulled out a small pistol and pressed it against my left temple.

"Robert, if I can't have you, I will kill us both. That way we both will be in heaven forever."

Images of my children and wife flashed before my eyes. I sensed death at the door. I told myself that I needed to stay alert and be wise about my next move. I think it finally hit me that she was mentally ill. And I believed she was crazy enough to pull the trigger and end my life.

I tried a soft approach. "I'm truly sorry, June, about how I've tried to push you away without considering your feelings. I care about you, but we need to find the best solution to the situation. Killing me won't help anyone."

She began to wail. The gun wavered. I grabbed her wrist and squeezed it hard until she dropped the gun on the floor. I snatched the pistol, feeling the cold metal in my shaking hand, and removed the bullets.

I jumped out of the car and leaned in the window. "Stay away from me and my family. If you ever come near me again, I'll call the cops."

After several days of not seeing her, I began to breathe a bit easier and thought June had finally gotten the message and would no longer bother me. If only . . .

Less than a week later, Sue and I were just pulling out of our subdivision to visit one of our members when I caught a glimpse of June in my rearview mirror. She had the audacity to follow us . . . again. Sue was driving, so I didn't hesitate to call the police.

When the police pulled her over, Sue and I stopped a distance from her. I will never forget June glaring at me with fire of hatred as she and her car were searched. The police warned her to stay away from us.

Meanwhile, June's lie about us was doing its work. The leader of the opposition group in the church saw this situation as a God-given opportunity to get rid of me. He drafted a willing June to his team.

Of course, I could no longer keep the "June situation" from Sue. The hardest thing I've ever had to do was to tell my wonderful wife about everything June had been doing and my ineffective efforts to get her to leave me alone. Sue didn't take it well. In fact, she was devastated. She had plenty to say, and I deserved everything she dished up. Suffice it to say, she could not believe that I would be that stupid and not tell her about June's misbehavior right from the start.

I handed in my resignation at the church and packed my bags. I determined to go to Austin so I could gather myself together. This was the lowest point in my life. I felt worthless. To add to my misery, our daughter rebelled and ran off to live with drug addicts.

I felt like the poster child for failure. I had failed everyone: the Lord, my wife, my children, and the congregation. Why in the world had I decided to quit a successful banking career and get into this mess? Was the inner voice I had been certain was God's just my imagination? Was the woman's prophecy about what I was to do a farce? I was fifty years old and had absolutely nothing to show for the past ten years of commitment and sacrifice.

While in Austin, I received many phone calls from the church members, including June, but I did not return any except Sue's. This served only to enrage June further. In retaliation, she concocted all kinds of stories about me. Mr. Hahn, the head of the opposition group, had exerted his influence on one of the Korean local newspapers to report in its headline: CHURCH SPLIT OVER PASTOR'S SEXUAL IMPROPRIETY. The article was totally one-sided, as it quoted only June's story and Hahn's comments.

I was embarrassed for putting my family through this. I considered contacting the paper to give my side of the story, but I quickly dismissed the idea. June and Hahn were bent on my destruction, and to respond to their lies would only draw out this unbearable situation and not settle anything. I chose instead to keep my head down and my mouth shut.

To make matters worse, some of my pastor friends started to distance themselves from me. In fact, one such pastor saw it as his opportunity to secure a position in the church. The local chapter of the Korean Baptist Association decided in my absence that I was guilty and voted to expel me from membership. As I was suffering, they did not come to my aid but poured salt in my wound. Why do Christians often refuse to show the same grace we receive? Why are we so quick to judge, to listen to and believe accusations without searching for the truth? Why do Christians kick their wounded instead of binding the wounds?

Alone. Humiliated. Failure. This is what I felt. After the horrid affair with Pearl S. Buck and Ted Harris was behind me, I thought I'd never find myself in this kind of situation again. But here I was. Different angle and different circumstances but similar feelings.

Unsuccessful as a senior pastor and feeling uncertain that I had been called into ministry in the first place, I questioned the veracity of the prophecy spoken to me by the woman at the Vineyard conference. I wondered if my years in seminary and in the pulpit had been a colossal waste of time.

However, several American pastors were eager to aid me. In particular, Jim Herrington, executive director of Union Baptist Association, supported me through prayer and a heavy dose of encouragement and counsel. But his kind words and actions did little to pull me out of the lowest point of my life.

I thank God Sue didn't turn her back on me. She and I went to Europe to get away together. I thought that visiting historic places there would take my mind off my misery. But it was December, and the cold, rainy weather in France and Italy did not seem to welcome us.

Even during some otherwise interesting guided tours, my mind drifted elsewhere. I ran through a list of career options, but each one seemed impossible to pursue. I had been away from banking for ten years, so to break in again would mean starting at the bottom. Doable, but I really didn't want to return to banking. I considered investing in real estate, but I didn't have the startup funds. I could work with Sue in our office-supply business, but there wasn't enough work available to warrant adding me to the staff.

The onslaught of darkness threatened to overwhelm me. I was in a pit that I saw no way out of. The only faint glimmer of hope I hung on to was the deep-in-my-soul belief in God's promise that He will make good come out of any circumstance for His own, who love Him and are called according to His purpose.

I didn't know what to expect when we returned to Houston three weeks later. I had hoped the dust had settled and I could figure out a way to rebuild my broken life.

Shortly after we arrived home, some of the still supportive church leaders informed me that, according to their count, two-thirds of the church members were on our side. I called my attorney friend from my banking days and told him everything. I learned from him that if we wanted, we could convene an assembly and vote to expel the one-third minority. He strongly urged that I do that.

I considered it, confident that I could win the vote and "redeem" myself. But I did not want to go through what appeared to be a potentially violent and protracted situation. I didn't want to be the instigator who forced a church to split. And for myself, I did not want to prolong the agony. I advised the deacons who were "on my side" that I had left the ministry for good and that I was returning to a secular profession—though I had no idea what that might be. That was my decision, and I was willing to live with it.

Those who were still in support of me started

to meet on their own every evening for prayer. The gathering picked up momentum and grew in numbers. They prayed until late into the night every evening and sought the guidance of the Holy Spirit. After about two weeks, almost all of them believed that the Spirit was telling them to leave the church and not contest the opposition. The deciding moment came when one of them stood up after much prayer and said, "The opposition is fighting us because they want the assets of the church—the buildings, the gym, the land, and the cash in the bank. That's why they are willing to fight to the death. But our pursuits are different. Are we not pursuing Jesus? Isn't Jesus everything to us? If so, all these assets don't mean anything. What are we still attached to?"

When I learned of this I could barely fathom it. I had already resigned from the church, but my pastor's heart ached over this situation. Why must fellow believers contend over assets? Over buildings and money? Temporal things? Jude verse 3 tells us that we Christians are to contend for the faith, not for worldly goods.

This revelation was like an epiphany for this small group of believers. Everyone realized the truth of what this person said. All voiced their desire to leave everything behind and start a new church comprised of people pursuing Jesus. The coming Sunday they would announce this to the whole church and walk out.

And that's exactly what they did, to the shock of all present for the worship service. Deacon Jae Kim read a prepared text that stated the group wanted to follow the voice of the Spirit and leave peacefully, giving up all rights to the assets of the church. The opposing party had earlier held their strategy sessions and was ready to engage in a nasty battle following the service that day. They were stunned but delighted that they had won without bloodshed.

The newly formed flock agreed to hold their first meeting at a Ramada Inn the following Sunday. They invited me to preach the first sermon.

I admit to being torn over this invitation. In my anguish of having to resign my position at the church, I had announced that I would no longer be a pastor and that I would be returning to banking. I hadn't consulted God over this hastily spoken decision. It was my wounded self who'd uttered those words.

Deep down, I had no desire to revive my banking career. I hoped that God's calling to be a pastor was still valid and active. He'd put within me a pastor's heart, which still beat, albeit weakly, within my breast.

This time I prayed about what I should say and do. I poured my heart out to God. I acted out 1 Peter 5:7 ("Cast all your anxiety on him because he cares for you") and threw every anxiety at God. I wanted to be rid of my cares and worries, and if He wanted them, I was glad to send them His way.

I got honest with God and confessed my error in not being open with Sue and the leadership of the church when faced with difficulties or problems. I repented of trying to solve the "June problem" on my own. I fasted and prayed a lot. I told Him I was sorry for hastily, and without consulting Him, announcing that I was leaving the pastorate and admitted that my heart's desire was to continue in the ministry.

The more I prayed, the more my relationship with God deepened. During these intimate hours with God, I began to sense His renewed call to a new path in the ministry. He gave me several ideas that I would later implement.

With a humble and serene heart, I accepted the invitation to preach at the Ramada Inn Sunday meeting. After the service, we gathered at Memorial Park and enjoyed a memorable picnic. I remember that it was an unusually mild, sunny day for December, perfect for a wonderful picnic. The joy and peace was evident in all those, even me, who pioneered New Life Baptist Church on December 19, 1999.

Yet all was not well with the world. The brewing fear of Y2K and the numerous unknowns associated with the new millennium loomed on the horizon.

Chapter Twenty-Six

———◆———

THE VISION

I DID NOT WANT TO BE A PASTOR WHO simply did "church." New Life seemed aimed in the right direction—following God's leading—but I did not want to repeat my past failure. Though I was confident that pastoring the New Life congregation was what God wanted me to do, I was stressed about knowing where I had gone amiss in my first church and how God would work it for my good. But I was certain that prayer and fasting were to be an integral part of knowing the *mahashaba*, God's blueprint for my life. I wanted more than the assurance that He was with me. I needed a clear purpose and direction I could commit my life to.

On the fifth day of fasting, I felt a strong impression in my heart.

"Plant one hundred churches for My kingdom!"

I shook my head and concluded it must have come from my own imagination. Here I was, struggling with just one church!

The next day I knelt down, prayed, and heard the same "voice."

"Plant one hundred churches for My kingdom!"

Half believing the command might be coming from the Lord, I wrote it down in my Day Planner. And then, the voice nudged me: *"Support one thousand missionaries!"*

I wrote that down quickly.

"Make ten thousand disciples!"

Again, I jotted that down.

"Win a hundred thousand souls!"

My first response was: "How can I do that, Lord? I have failed You with just one church!"

And then He made me feel like Jeremiah by reminding me of the exchange in the first chapter of the book he authored: "Do not say you are a youth, because everywhere I send you, you shall go, and all that I command you, you shall speak."

He did not want my excuses.

I shared this with Sue, who, as always, was supportive of my efforts for the Lord. She expressed full confidence in this vision and encouraged me to start the new ministry.

In New Life's next worship service, I boldly declared that this vision from the Lord would be the goal of this church. Some members were understandably skeptical, but most of them were enthusiastic and supportive.

I taught from the Bible on what kind of church New Life would aspire to be. Many have taught the Jerusalem church as the ideal model for churches to emulate. Acts 2:42–47 describes the atmosphere of that church:

It grew numerically: three thousand were added in one day.

The members devoted themselves to the teachings of the apostles.

There was a true *koinonia*, in which they broke bread and shared meals.

They were committed to prayer.

They sold their possessions and goods and gave to anyone in need.

This church had everything. What would anyone possibly add to this? This was the picture of heaven on earth, and no other church in Christendom has been as this one in Jerusalem. But I saw one critical piece missing in this picture. Just look at the two commands Jesus made to the disciples right before He ascended into heaven: "Therefore go and make disciples of all nations, baptizing them in the name of the Father and of the Son and of the Holy Spirit, and teaching them to obey everything I have commanded you" (Matt. 28:19–20); "But you will receive power when the Holy Spirit comes on you; and you will be my witnesses in Jerusalem, and in all Judea and Samaria, and to the ends of the earth" (Acts 1:8).

In both of these commands, which may be construed as Jesus's last will and testament, He stressed for the gospel to reach the Gentiles of all nations. The Jerusalem church did a great job of doing all the right things for a church except for this crucial part of Jesus's commission. Many churches today are like the Jerusalem church—they are more focused on their "church building" rather than on "kingdom building."

The martyrdom of Stephen was not accidental. Acts 11:19 clearly indicates that it was the turning point at which the saints in Jerusalem were forced to scatter, some landing in Antioch. There they reached several different nationalities, including the Greeks, Romans, and even some Africans (13:1). The citizens in Antioch had a favorable impression of these Jesus followers and dubbed them "Christians" for the first time. The Christians were impacting the secular world in a broad sense.

When the apostles in Jerusalem heard of Gentiles receiving the Holy Spirit upon believing in Jesus, they sent Barnabas to confirm it. It is interesting that at this time the apostles thought it odd that God would anoint Gentiles with the Holy Spirit. Barnabas was pleasantly surprised to witness this phenomenon and encouraged the members to cling to Jesus. Barnabas was so overwhelmed with what he saw that he didn't believe he could lead this church on his own. He went to Tarsus and brought back Paul, who joined in the work of the Holy Spirit there for a year.

The Antioch church is also the first church in the Bible to have commissioned missionaries. Both Paul and Barnabas were sent away in obedience to the Great Commission. They were definitely kingdom building and not church building. The Antioch church had everything that the Jerusalem church did plus the most important aspect of the Great Commission: they reached the Gentiles. The turning point in Christianity's history was made in Antioch. This is the model church New Life members wanted to emulate: about fifty Koreans with the vision of eventually building our church from different ethnic groups who were sold out to reach the world with the name of Christ.

But there was a problem.

Chapter Twenty-Seven

———•———

THE FRUIT

AFTER HOLDING OUR FIRST SERVICE IN A Ramada Inn conference room, which was costly, we found a building to meet in where the owner graciously offered it at a low rental price. It was a party hall attached to a sushi restaurant and had a large space with a stage that would work perfectly as a pulpit. It even had a dance floor with a psychedelic disco ball.

Before services on Sunday mornings, our leaders had to clean up the place from the previous night's party. No wonder the rent was so cheap. The owner got a cleaning crew who paid for the privilege! But we were so grateful to have a place to worship, no one complained while sweeping up stinky cigarette butts and gathering empty beer cans. We joined in the name of our Lord and invited the Holy Spirit to come into our midst. Surely His presence was there.

But our joy of using the space lasted less than a

month, when the owner left me a terse, handwritten note saying we would have to vacate. He didn't give any reasons, and we wondered why he didn't tell me in person. Something didn't seem right.

I immediately went next door to his restaurant, but he was nowhere to be seen. I found his wife and asked her why we were being asked to leave. Had we done something to offend him? At first she was hesitant to say anything. But after some probing, she admitted that someone was pressuring her husband to quit renting to us. He wasn't happy about it, but he felt he had no choice. I knew intuitively who that was. The owner was a member of the church whose pastor was antagonistic about my ministry. I couldn't help but conclude that the pastor had pressured this guy to kick us out.

New Life took the matter to prayer. We went on our knees, once again pouring out our feelings of helplessness yet not feeling sorry for ourselves. Instead, the situation forced us to cry out to the Lord in desperation and dependence.

Some of the leaders and I immediately began looking for a suitable meeting place. I first contacted over thirty mostly Anglo churches in the area and appealed for some space to rent. Unfortunately, most of the pastors would not return calls or even agree to see me. And then a break came when I stumbled upon an old gymnasium that had been vacant for several years.

As it turned out, this was where Mary Lou Retton, 1984 Olympic gold medal winner, with her famed coach Bela Karolyi, had practiced for the Olympics. It had about 20,000 feet of wide-open space and a huge, unused pit filled with filthy, stagnant water. Cobwebs hung everywhere. It would've been a fantastic setting for a spooky movie. And it was perfect for us!

The landlord told us to take it "as is," because he wasn't going to give any building allowances. The best he would do was give us three months of free rent, then after that we'd have to pay $4,000 a month. Our deacons quickly calculated that to fix up the place and put in a sanctuary, classrooms, and a fellowship hall would cost about $100,000. We didn't have any money, but we believed that God would somehow provide everything we needed.

The members generously gave of their money, time, and talents to transform the old gym. Several came straight there after work and labored for hours. The ladies cooked while the men worked. We all took a break for dinner, sitting around piles of sheetrock on the concrete floor. At those times of fellowship, we shared much laughter and unity.

On Sundays and Wednesdays, we set up chairs and held worship services next to the piles of construction materials and unfinished walls, but we had joy and gratitude as we worshipped our living Lord. We completed the construction in fifty-six days, just four days more than it took Nehemiah to rebuild the walls in Jerusalem.

And we enjoyed fruit of our short ministry as well.

One of the Korean members was dating a Vietnamese man, Jeff, who was only twelve years old when he and his parents fled Vietnam on an overcrowded boat. The people had little food and water to share as they endlessly drifted toward Thailand. As though their agony was not enough, pirates attacked, taking what few possessions they had. Most of the men were left with only their underwear. But by the grace of God, they survived and eventually made their way to the United States.

December 31, 1999, was the first New Year's Eve for New Life to celebrate as a congregation. We worshipped all evening and into the wee hours of the morning. As the clock struck midnight, we offered our first prayer of the New Year. We gave our aspirations to the Lord as well as our financial offerings as firstfruits.

That year we began a tradition that we hold to this day. Each member wrote his or her prayer requests on an index card. As each family came forward to be prayed over, they handed me their cards. In the following days, I made copies of the cards for the pastoral staff so we could pray over them every day during the year. Toward the end of the year, I mailed the cards back to their owners, who often gave amazing testimonies as to how God faithfully answered their prayers.

It was almost 2:00 in the morning of the New Year when Jeff and his girlfriend came up for prayer. They were the last for me to pray over, since all other families had left. It was obvious to me that he had something on his mind.

"How can I pray for you, Jeff?"

He shuffled a bit, then with a trembling voice he said, "I want to accept Jesus as my Lord. Would you help me?"

What a way to start the New Year! After asking some questions to determine his understanding of his decision, I explained the core of the gospel message. I then led him to the Lord. A few days later, I had the honor of baptizing him, and then later I officiated the couple's wedding. Jeff progressed in his faith, and a few years later he felt called into the ministry. He enrolled in Southwestern Baptist Seminary and eventually became an ordained minister.

The church was slowly but steadily growing by adding more members like Jeff, who were willing to be discipled as workers for the kingdom. Every time we gathered for worship or prayer, we repeated our vision, which had become the goal of New Life. We wanted to win souls, make disciples of them, and send them out to plant churches.

Though we were advancing our vision, we were not without opposition. One of the deacons who worked very hard in remodeling the church began behaving erratically. Sometimes he exploded in violent anger over trivial matters. And then he began to dictate to me how I should run the church. I tried to be diplomatic, but I remained firm about not compromising my beliefs in the direction of our church. One Sunday, he broke out in a rage. He kicked a stand-up fan to pieces and walked out, taking two other families with him.

This was, of course, very upsetting, not only to me but to the congregation. I dared not try to analyze his behavior other than to conclude that this was a demonstration of his flawed character. I've learned over the years that a pastor must deal with all kinds of personalities while running a church, which can be difficult at times. But I've also learned that following God as He directs His church is the only way to lead a congregation.

Chapter Twenty-Eight

———•———

DREAM VERSUS VISION

ONE OF THE STORIES I ENJOY SHARING is about the time Mother Teresa held a news conference in India to reveal the plan to build an orphanage with a hospital attached to it. Those who came to hear this exciting news were impressed with the grand scale of the project and how it could benefit not only the orphanage but also the community. One of the reporters shot a question to Mother Teresa. "A project of this magnitude would require millions of dollars. How much money do you have in the bank?"

Her answer left reporters speechless—an incredibly difficult thing to do. "Three dollars."

They chuckled at themselves for falling for what they perceived as this great woman's joke.

Then Mother Teresa clarified her answer. "All I need to make this project possible is the three dollars, faith in God, and a vision. These three are the keys to success."

We often hear about the importance of having a dream. Visit Amazon.com and you'll find a vast number of titles on reaching your dreams. We also hear a lot about fulfilling your vision. Many use the terms *dream* and *vision* interchangeably. Is there a difference? If so, what differentiates a dreamer from a visionary? Many people dream dreams, and they are what they are—dreams, what you fantasize and wish for. One can dream about becoming a millionaire, while another dreams of marrying a movie star. But most of these end up being just dreams or fantasies and serve no particular purpose. They rarely benefit humanity or God's kingdom.

Visions, however, are different. They have a specific purpose and benefit others or help to expand God's kingdom. Abraham, Jacob, Joseph, and Nehemiah are good biblical examples of visionaries. They all had one thing in common: They did not dream up their own visions but received them from God. Abraham was told that he would be the father of all nations, and he knew this would come true when Jesus would come to save the world. "Your father Abraham rejoiced at the thought of seeing my day; he saw it and was glad" (John 8:56).

Abraham did not invent his own vision by dreaming up something he wished; rather, the vision came from God. Abraham believed it, possessed it, and even "saw" it. As a result, he had much joy.

I taught our congregation the importance of having this kind of vision. Every time we gathered for worship, I reminded them about the vision God gave to our church and that we should "see" the end result and rejoice in it. If the vision came from God, it would not be up to us to accomplish it, but He would certainly make it happen. True vision is God-given, God-directed, and God-accomplished. Anything else is mere fantasy or dreams that vanish as quickly as they come.

This concept has become foundational to our congregation as we responded to God's leading in ways we never thought possible.

Chapter Twenty-Nine

————◆————

HAVANA

WHILE I WAS STILL AT MY FIRST pastorate, John Lee and I were exploring ministry opportunities in Cuba. On a late winter morning in 1998, I pulled aside the drapes of my room in the Melia Cohiba Hotel, Havana, Cuba, to a stunning panoramic view of the sea. Straight north, Key West, Florida, lay a mere ninety miles away. A short distance as the crow flies, but the countries of Cuba and the United States are far greater separated by political and religious ideology, as well as their philosophies of individual freedom for their people. So much so that many Cuban citizens have given up all their worldly possessions, left family and friends, and risked their lives to cross the Straits of Florida in their pursuit of establishing a new life in America. Not all were successful. Too many met with tragedies. You hear many such stories in Cuba.

John and I had arrived in Havana late the night before. Though it is illegal for Americans to travel to Cuba, John told me about the possibility of entering the country via Mexico. As we rode in the hotel van from the airport, I tried to get my first glimpses of Cuba, but the streets were dimly lit, so I couldn't see much of anything. Most of the cities I have flown into have brightly lit airport expressways leading to the downtown area, but not here. Instead, the dark roads were in dire need of repairs. The roadside buildings looked old and unmaintained since the revolution, when in 1959 Fidel Castro took control of the government and established a socialistic state, which eventually reformed into a Communistic state. The driver zigzagged around numerous bicycles and horse buggies with no tail lights, miraculously getting us to the hotel without killing anyone.

Arriving at the hotel, we seemed to have entered a different country. We drove into a well-lighted circular driveway, where a uniformed doorman met us. Attached to the hotel was a lively disco. Tall, good-looking girls milled about, wearing tight, short skirts. Evidently, I had incorrectly assumed that Cubans were generally poor, for these young ladies were dressed like upper-class kids. Later I learned that my original assumption had been correct and that these gals were prostitutes catering to the tourists.

It wasn't until the next morning that we were able to get out and see Havana. Though it was the middle of February, John and I had no need for jackets or sweaters. In fact, the sun beat down on our heads. I walked across Malecón, the boulevard that winds around the seashore, and encountered several young Cubans sitting along the seawall, chitchatting. Some were fishing with just the lines tied to a stick. One of the young men happened to speak some English.

I introduced myself then asked, "What kind of work do you do? Are you a college student?"

He smirked. "Only the privileged go to college, for which the government pays the entire costs, including books and dormitory expenses. They do so only to train and groom future Communist leaders. Me? I am unemployed. I do odd jobs as they occasionally crop up."

"How about the distribution of necessities by the government?" I inquired.

He gave a mirthless laugh and scowled. He pulled out a well-worn coupon book from his pocket. "You see these rationing coupons? This one allows me to buy a pair of shoes, and this one a pair of pants. As far as food, I receive a handful of rice and beans each week. Occasionally I get some sugar, but never do I get soap, toothpaste, or other necessities. One day soon even the rice and beans will disappear." He gazed north across the water, as though his future lay there in the distance and not here. "We have no future in this country. The one thing we receive frequently from the government is empty promises. No one believes in it anymore."

As we headed back to the hotel I stopped another young man. "*Dónde encuentro una iglesia?*"

I tried my best Spanish, wanting to know about a church nearby. I guess I made myself understood, for he motioned for us to follow him. It turned out to be about a three-mile trek toward downtown. This was the first Cuban kindness we had experienced. Sweat had drenched our clothing by the time we arrived at a massive Methodist church that Americans had built about a hundred years before. A lot of young people were hanging around, waiting for the Wednesday evening service to begin. It would seem many Cubans have one thing in abundance—time.

We learned quickly that these people are not in a hurry to begin anything, including the service. We had to leave behind our American perception of time. When the worship finally got off the ground, it was fast-paced and uplifting, with a lot of Caribbean instruments. It was marvelous and lasted almost an hour. A black man in his twenties sitting next to us volunteered to translate for us. I had to concentrate so hard to decipher what he was saying in his heavily accented English that my head hurt.

After the service, I wanted to spend some time with the young people and find out about their lives and thoughts, so I invited them to some ice cream. The word spread quickly, and all of a sudden, we were entertaining a group of fifteen young people.

Rather than the ice cream, most of them ordered pizza, a rare treat for them. A bright-looking girl with brown hair and blue eyes recommended I try the chocolate ice cream. "Did you know that Cuba has the best ice cream in the world?" Delusion is free, even in North Korea, as we Koreans like to say. I complied so as not to disappoint her, but I reserve my judgment on the "best ice cream in the world" claim.

This young lady's name was Monica. She was eager to explain anything I wanted to know about Cuba. She was twenty-one and lived with her mother and a brother. Her dad had recently passed away. She spoke no English, but her best friend, Anna, happily volunteered to translate. The girls offered to be our guides to Havana.

The next morning, Monica and Anna met us in our hotel lobby. Monica had our schedule written down on a piece of paper. She told us that she had asked the Holy Spirit for guidance early that morning before she came up with the list. Her eyes sparkled with genuine excitement and joy. It was apparent she was in love with the Lord. I was grateful that we were able to meet her so soon in Cuba.

We first invited them to have breakfast with us on the second floor of the hotel before embarking on our itinerary. When the waitress placed the food before us, Monica's eyes went round and lit up as though a light had been switched on. She said that she had never seen such a variety of foods and in such quantity. Before taking a bite of her breakfast, she rolled some of the food items in napkins and stuffed them in her purse to take home. Anna explained that an average Cuban subsists on not much more than rice and beans. Beef is banned for the Cubans, because it is reserved for the tourists. They joked that it's a bigger crime to run over a cow than a Cuban. The cows are not only sacred in India, but here in Cuba also, as they all belong to Fidel Castro.

The first place they took us to was the home of an old pastor, who was about seventy years old and had converted his house into a church. He had suffered much persecution since the revolution of 1959, but he told us that things had gotten a little easier since Pope John Paul's visit in 1996. His previous living room, now the sanctuary, had a high ceiling and wood floors. It was sparsely furnished with a small podium, sound system, and folding chairs stacked up against the walls. He said on a typical Sunday he would have more than fifty worshippers stuffed into this small place, but some inevitably had to stand outside looking in through the windows. He was using the kitchen for Sunday school, and right above it was the loft he had built for a bedroom. I was struck by this godly man's humility.

As we were about to leave after a tearful prayer, he rolled up one of his trouser legs and showed a gruesome sight. Black veins that looked as though they were about to burst protruded from his calves.

He pulled a wrinkled prescription out of his wallet. "I cannot get this prescription filled because such medicine does not exist in Cuba. Would you please bring it the next time you come?"

I took the worn paper and gave him my solemn promise.

Monica, under the direction of the Holy Spirit, had introduced us to a typical house church in Cuba, and later we would visit many other house churches throughout Cuba.

The way Monica always consulted the Holy Spirit before every little decision impressed me. At first I thought it was a little corny, but later I realized how this was a natural part of her life. She expressed a genuine interest and love for the soul of every person she encountered. She didn't hesitate to share her testimony and then invite the person to receive Christ. Even when we were in taxicabs, she lovingly witnessed to the cabbies and even led one driver tearfully to the Lord.

Her vigor shamed and challenged John and me.

We were also touched when Anna told us that someone had given Monica a used TV, but she gave it away to a poor little boy in the neighborhood who could not watch his favorite cartoons. She had no greed whatsoever for material things. She was always thinking of others who had fewer possessions than she did.

Monica invited us to her apartment. I tried to hide my horror as we walked in. Her living conditions were truly appalling. The complex was run down and dark. Her bedroom consisted of a mattress on the floor. The kitchen windows had no glass. Needless to say, no one in her household had a steady source of income.

On the last day of our four-day visit, Monica took us to an industrial area of Havana. We hopped into a cab that dodged the potholes of the dark and dingy streets and alleys. We stopped at a church that met in someone's backyard. A few makeshift wooden benches sat haphazardly on cement blocks. The podium was fashioned from a fruit box. Only a handful gathered to worship with us. Monica led the singing a cappella, and a young couple who arrived on a bicycle delivered the message. Later John and I were stunned to learn that they would pedal over twelve miles one way to come to this small gathering.

John and I couldn't help but acknowledge how truly we were blessed. We had jobs, we never had to wonder if we'd have enough food for the next meal, and we gave little thought to the clothing that filled our closets and drawers. We could not leave without sharing from our bounty, so we left $300 with the owner who was hosting this church to put a tin roof over the backyard.

Chapter Thirty

―――◆―――

MONICA

ABOUT THREE MONTHS AFTER THE SHORT but unforgettable trip to Cuba, I received an urgent phone call from Anna. She said Monica had fallen ill and was hospitalized. She handed the phone to a Cuban doctor who lived and practiced in Canada but was visiting his family there. He said Monica was suffering from a rare blood disease, which could be fatal if not treated quickly. He said the medicine she required was not available in Cuba. He would write the prescription, which was manufactured by Abbot Laboratories and some pharmaceutical company in Finland, and fax it to us. I immediately contacted my brother-in-law, a neurologist in Houston, to see if he could help speed up the process by writing a prescription, but to my disappointment, he explained it would be illegal for him to prescribe the medication without having seen the patient.

I contacted the manufacturer, but they offered no help. As a last resort, John Lee found a pharmacist who was willing to order the medicine for us. We were anxious to get this delivered to Monica, but the process seemed to take forever. We couldn't send it directly to Cuba because of the embargo, so we had to send it first to Canada, and then from Canada to Cuba.

Though it didn't take forever to get to Cuba, it did arrive too late to save Monica's life. This news devastated me. I struggled to make sense of why—why we couldn't get the medicine to her in time, why someone so on fire for the Lord was taken home, why I couldn't do more.

She left a handwritten memo addressed to me, her Papa Chino.

My Papa Chino:

As you know I am in the hospital, and the doctor from Canada tells me I need medication that is not available in Cuba. I don't put my trust in medicine but in my Lord, who can heal me if He wants to. As Paul said, "To live is Christ, and to die is gain." Either way, it's a blessing.

I am grateful to the Lord for getting to know you, and although it's been a short while, I know you have replaced my dad, who departed from us a few years ago. He was very handsome and gentle, just like you, and so much in love with the Lord, just like you.

Whether we see each other again or not, I pray we will continue to proclaim the most precious name of our Lord, Jesus Christ.

In Christ,

Your Cuban daughter, Monica

My short visit to Cuba, connecting with the home churches, meeting and then losing Monica—these things worked together to begin the chapter of my life in Cuba that God was authoring.

Chapter Thirty-One

CUBA

AFTER MONICA'S DEATH AND MY resignation from my first church, I had no choice but to set aside plans for serving the Cuban Christian community. Once New Life was established and we had finished remodeling the gym into a suitable church building, I revived the Cuban ministry. The first step was to contact one of the house pastors Monica had introduced to me and determine if we could work together to strengthen the Cuban believers and saturate Castro's country with the gospel message.

Pastor Raul Fernandez, who preferred to be called "Paul," was a silver-haired man whom I thought was much older than I was. It turns out that he's several years younger! Evidently, his hard life had aged him.

Converted when he was nineteen, he did some time in the penitentiary for preaching the gospel. Now with his wife and two grown daughters, he lived in a row house, in which he converted the downstairs into a chapel. When I met him, he was in the middle of adding concrete blocks to put in living quarter upstairs for his family. Two beds and an old bookcase separated the rooms. As in Monica's house, none of the windows had panes. The glassless kitchen window looked out over a nearby garbage pit. Stench and dust freely dominated the rooms.

When I first met Pastor Paul, he greeted me with big smiles and surprised me by cracking some jokes about Castro. Later, I learned that Cubans poke fun at their leaders in an effort to make light of their severe conditions.

The present circumstance Paul and his family were living under took my breath away. He'd recently had appendix surgery, and I could not believe the sloppy way a mere bandage and gauze were applied to the incision. His wife was short and stocky, and her small, deformed feet made walking awkward. She asked if I could bring more comfortable shoes next time I came to Cuba.

Paul had about fifty members in his congregation. He did just about everything in the church. He led music, preached, prayed, and cleaned the bathrooms. His daughters were part of the worship band. At our first meeting, he offered to let me preach.

"Thank you, Paul, but I don't want to get you in

trouble with the law."

"It will be an honor to go to jail again for the Lord," he said.

So I delivered a message titled "My Food" based on John 4:34. While the disciples considered the food they ate, Jesus said His food was to do the will of the Father who sent Him. It appeared many were genuinely responding to the challenge of shifting focus from carnal desires to the spiritual tasks at hand.

After the service, I asked Paul what he thought was most needed for the churches in Cuba. What he said piqued my interest, because his answer was exactly what I had struggled with during my dozen trips to Chile.

"What we need is something, or someone, that will stay here for a long time. The problem with you foreigners is that you come and do a short stint of preaching the gospel to the ones who don't need it because they are not baby Christians. Most of you drop a few dollars and don't come back or stay in contact. There is no connection or continuity. That's why we Cubans have been doing it alone all these years."

"Can you give me some specific examples of what you need that will make a lasting difference?" I sat on the edge of my seat, waiting for his answer.

"What we need is quality training for the workers. We have very few seminaries and not many can afford to attend them. Enrollment is limited because of government restrictions. We need a school where people can freely come and learn and be trained to do God's work in our churches."

This struck a chord deep within me. This plan was what I had been praying about for Chile but had to abort because I could not find a suitable partner. As Paul and I discussed various ideas, we decided we'd first do a three-day seminar for the house-church pastors on my next trip. Paul would host it in his home, and I would pick up the tab for food and transportation for the attendees.

I could hardly contain my excitement as I returned to Houston and began to organize the next trip. Since we were headed into summer, college would be out of session. We took eight college students, plus Sue and I went, for a total of ten.

A few days before our departure, I received a call from Jay Lee, the deacon who'd kicked the fan to pieces and left our church. He said, "Mr. Park, I hear you are going to Cuba. I am warning you to stay away from there. You have no business there." His words were peppered with the vilest words.

Why was he calling to tell me this? Why the foul language? And he intentionally called me *mister* instead of *pastor* just to insult me.

"No one but God can tell me what to do when it

comes to doing God's work," I said.

"I am telling you," he said, his voice rising as he again cursed at me, "if you go, something bad is going to happen. I promise you!" He hung up.

I summoned the parents of the students who had signed up to go and explained the situation. I had to tell them that it was illegal to visit Cuba, and I could not guarantee their safety. If they decided not to send their kids, I would certainly understand. But without hesitation, one by one they said they would still send them. After all, they were doing God's work, and He would assume responsibility for them. I was touched by their trust in the Lord, yet I still felt the weight of responsibility on my shoulders in case something went wrong.

Off to Cuba we went.

The trip was a success! About 300 Cuban college students gathered in a city called Morón. We ministered to them by offering seminars and workshops. One afternoon, we challenged them to go in pairs and knock on every door and present the gospel or invite them to the evening service. The students were excited and could not wait to give praise reports about the many people who responded to the message and invitation.

I brought the sermons in the evening services. To this day, I remember how moved I was to see about a dozen deaf people praising God with their hands. I prayed for all who were present, and many fell on the floor and basked in the presence of the Holy Spirit.

Back in Havana in Paul's house, we held a teaching seminar for pastors of underground churches. To my surprise, we had over one hundred pastors crammed into the room. We were so jam-packed, the pulpit from which I taught pressed against the knees of the pastors in the front row. We were all dripping in sweat because of so many bodies stuffed into the small room, but no one seemed to mind. People were even standing outside, looking in the windows.

Midway through the seminar, some pastors sitting in the back interrupted my teaching. "Three soldiers who were passing by heard your message. They want to know if they can receive the Lord into their hearts before moving on!"

A nurse in her white uniform and cap also came forward with them. I had Paul lead them in a salvation prayer.

Toward the end of the sessions, I led the group in prayer. When I laid my hand on each of them, the Spirit worked in such a powerful way that no one would know I was a Baptist minister. I appeared more like a Pentecostal. That day, the Lord made it very clear where He was taking us from that point on.

Another highlight on that trip was our visit to a church led by a black pastor who preferred to be called

"Frank." The church was large enough to accommodate over a hundred comfortably. It was the result of Pastor Frank's continued effort to extend his house, even taking up both the front and back yards. A tremendous sense of excitement and passion permeated the air as we walked into the middle of their worship. We felt challenged by the intensity of anticipation that God would do something great for them that evening.

I preached "You Can Do Greater Things" based on John 14:12–14 and Matthew 14:22–32. I asked, "How is it that out of the twelve, Peter was the only one to walk on water? What happened to the eleven who took comfort inside the boat? Are you willing to take a risk like Peter, or are you like the rest of the disciples in the boat?"

The members responded enthusiastically. "We want to be like Peter!"

After the message, I invited those who were willing to lay down their lives for the Lord to come forward. The entire congregation, including Frank and his wife, came to the front. I laid my hands on them, and people were falling everywhere. The attendees' anticipation increased almost to the point of frenzy. I was intentionally careful not to manipulate the situation so as not to get in the way of the Holy Spirit. I tried to flow with the Spirit and just wanted to be the "pencil" in the hands of God.

And then someone pushed close to me a man sitting in a wheelchair. He seemed very old and frail, although I later learned he was only fifty years old. He lifted his gaze to me, and I could clearly see hope in his eyes rimmed with dark circles.

"How long have you been confined to the wheelchair?" I asked.

"Seven years!" the person pushing the wheelchair snapped before the man could answer.

"Is he able to walk at all?"

"No, he can't."

Suddenly I felt helpless and searched for some kind of an escape. They had no doubts that this man would receive healing through my hand, but I had plenty. My desire not to disappoint them was so strong that I felt I somehow had to find a way out of this without losing face.

Then while I was still hoping for an answer that would get me out of this, out of my mouth came the next question. "Do you have faith that God will heal you?"

Without hesitation, he said unequivocally, "Sí!"

Now I had no choice but to lay my hands on him.

While praying silently, asking the Lord to take charge, I blurted, "In the name of Jesus Christ of Nazareth, I command you to get up and walk!"

By this point the crowd had reached a passion that I

normally would have shied away from. They screamed and yelled, fully expecting a miracle to happen.

And it did.

The old man at first struggled to get out of his chair. Then he stood. He took a few shuffling, uncertain steps. The more steps he took, the stronger his legs became, as well as his confidence. Then he sent the congregation into an uproar as he ran the full length of the church, back and forth. He started to leap and dance with joy! No one in that room had dry eyes. Tears streamed down our faces as we praised our wonderful Lord Jesus.

While I was ecstatic at this miracle, I was also humbled that the Lord would use me to bring healing to this man. God never wastes an opportunity to accomplish His will, and I believe God healed this man not only for his benefit but also for me so as to deepen my trust in His power.

Then our time to leave Cuba and return home was upon us. We were so blessed by the experience that we had forgotten the intimidation Jay Lee laid on us before we embarked on this trip.

When we arrived in Houston, Texas, at the George Bush Intercontinental Airport via Cancun, a customs agent was waiting for us. He ordered our entourage to stand in one line and confronted me first.

"Where are you all coming from?"

"Cancun, Mexico," I replied.

"How about before that?"

"What do you mean before that? We are returning from our trip to Cancun, Mexico," I said.

"Did you not go to Cuba? Yes or no? And you'd better not lie, or you will be in big trouble." The officer fairly snarled at me.

Cuban immigration does not stamp your passport. You buy a tourist card in Cancun, which allows entrance into Cuba; therefore, there was no physical evidence that we had been to Cuba. I had no doubt that Lee had informed the Immigration Department of our travels to Cuba. Lying seemed futile at that point.

The officer cited the Cuban Embargo Act of 1963 and said we could be fined up to a million dollars or ten years in prison for violating it. I was not worried about myself. In fact, I would be honored to suffer for the Lord. But I was more concerned about the students, some of whom were not US citizens and possessed only a student visa or green card. They could be easily deported. Adding to the potential tragedy was that two of the girls traveling with us were Jay Lee's nieces. His fierce hatred for me would even put at risk the lives of his own family.

I silently prayed, *Lord, You said all things come together for good for those who love You and have been called for Your purpose. We are those people. Please bring good out of this situation. You are the only One who is able to do that.*

I begged the officer to let the students go and deal with me however he saw fit. He studied me then perused the faces of the young people. He worked his jaw while reviewing his paperwork, occasionally glancing up to scowl at me.

"I will let you go this time. But be assured that this information will be put into our system. If you violate the embargo again, we will exercise the full force of the law. Now, wait here."

He left the room and returned a few minutes later with several sheets of paper. He shoved them at me. I glanced down and read the title: COMPREHENSIVE GUIDELINES FOR LICENSE APPLICATIONS TO ENGAGE IN TRAVEL-RELATED TRANSACTIONS INVOLVING CUBA. He explained how I could apply for a license from the Treasury Department to travel to Cuba legally for religious purposes.

Oh, how we rejoiced! The Lord defeated the Devil again and made us prevail. This reminded me of what Joseph said to his brothers in Genesis 50:20: "You intended to harm me, but God intended it for good to accomplish what is now being done, the saving of many lives."

Chapter Thirty-Two

---◆---

LEARNING INSTITUTE OF TEXAS

Another ministry God gave New Life Baptist Church in Houston was to offer classes to our community, such as computer basics, Spanish, and English as a Second Language (ESL). The program was an instant hit and enticed many unbelievers from the community to set their feet on the church grounds. We prayed that this ministry would give us the opportunity not only to help them with these essential needs but also to witness Christ to attendees.

My original vision was for our church to create a Life Center for the community, providing services the people required to make their lives a bit easier and richer. Aside from the educational courses, I thought about providing free legal help, since many were undocumented immigrants who lived in constant fear of being picked up and deported. They neither knew who to turn to nor had any resources to get help. I also considered providing free medical services if I could find volunteer doctors and nurses. Providing facilities for various sports, music lessons, and a food pantry were among some of the ideas I had so that the folks in the community came to church to fulfill their basic necessities.

But I quickly found out that reality posed far more and greater challenges than we could handle. Lack of volunteers, financial resources, and suitable facilities were some of the major issues we faced. Missing even one of these criteria rendered the goal impossible. Consequently, we had to cancel one service after another. But out of all the classes, ESL was the most in demand, so we kept that one going. In fact, it eventually evolved into helping foreign students in a more systematic and academic way.

This gave birth to The Learning Institute of Texas (LIT) in 2001. It also entailed separating this ministry from New Life and forming a nonprofit corporation, allowing the school to provide quality education to foreign nationals legally. We put together a board of directors, who applied with the Department of Homeland Security so that LIT could issue I-20 forms—Certificate of Eligibility for Nonimmigrant (F-1) Student Status for Academic and Language Students—and recruit students from overseas. In 2002, DHS granted us this license, and we focused on developing the best methods to teach ESL to those who desired to advance to college or graduate school. We began with about twenty Korean students. As of this writing, LIT has over 200 students representing twenty different nationalities.

Though our ideas were good and helped many, God had a much greater plan for LIT. When talking and praying with Pastor Paul and other Cuban pastors, I felt strongly that the Lord was leading us to start a Bible training institute in Havana. This came about after we held several teaching sessions for the pastors of underground churches.

Although I was moved by their passion and zeal for the Lord, I was equally concerned about their lack of education. Some of them had difficulty taking notes of my lectures. But more alarming was that these pastors lacked knowledge of basic theology and hermeneutics. When I asked a few how they prepared their sermons, I cringed when many answered that they shared testimonies and interpreted the Bible passages the way they'd heard or read somewhere. Of course, most of them wanted to receive theological training but, unfortunately, could not because of limited space in the seminaries. Most important, they simply could not afford to enroll in the schools.

In the ensuing strategy meetings I had with Pastor Paul and other leaders, we decided to use LIT as the training institute's name, because the Cubans liked it and its logo. We targeted April 1, 2002, as opening day for our school and decided on a two-year course that covered most of the basic subjects taught in a typical seminary.

But then the big question arose: how to advertise our school. Being a Communist country, Cuba had only one newspaper, *Granma*, which is the official Communist paper. (*Granma* is the name of the yacht that brought Fidel Castro and his rebels to the shores of Cuba, which triggered the revolution.) We would dare not advertise our illegal operation, nor would the paper accept any advertising from a Christian organization. That left us with only one option: word of mouth. I asked the pastors to do their best to spread the word about the school opening.

Meanwhile, I flew back to Houston.

Upon returning home, I mobilized the whole church in Houston to pray that LIT Cuba would have at least twelve applicants. After all, Jesus had that many disciples. It would be a good start for us. Furthermore, because no Cuban pastor could afford to pay the tuition, New Life would cover the costs, but we were financially limited and could not afford to sponsor any more than twelve enrollees.

A few months later, two deacons from New Life and I went to Cuba for the institute's launch. We also took two new Yamaha keyboards and other electronic equipment donated to the Cuban institute. Though we knew the equipment might be confiscated, the institute certainly could use it, so we figured the risk was worth it.

We were not able to put the keyboards in any kind of suitcase because of the sheer size, especially the length, so we carried them in the original boxes. When we stood in line in immigration, we tried to hide our nervousness. The keyboard boxes broadcast what we were bringing into the country.

We watched as the customs officers opened *all* the luggage of the folks in front of us. I glanced at my deacons. We knew were in trouble. Their shoulders sagged and their eyes were downcast, not from weariness of the trip but from their obvious feelings of helplessness and hopelessness. I whispered to them to pray. I heard Deacon Jae Kim praying ever so faintly in tongues.

In less than a few minutes, an official emerged from a side door and marched straight toward us. He glanced over the boxes and asked me something in Spanish, which I couldn't understand. I explained to him in English that the equipment was a gift to our friends in Cuba. I felt certain he didn't understand a word of what I'd said, but what else could I do? I expected at any moment to be stripped of the keyboards and other electronics.

But then he motioned us to go on! We surely understood what that meant and wheeled our stuff out of that area in a snap, praising the Lord for answering our prayers so supernaturally. We were able to deliver the keyboards to two different house churches. Their worship became even livelier!

As a side note, a few years later, Sue and I spent a night at Pastor Isaiah's house in Santo Domingo, Cuba, and found the familiar keyboard box lying against the wall of his bedroom. He said he would not part with it, for it was a symbol of a miracle gift from God.

Finally, LIT Cuba's opening day arrived. We started early in the morning, believing in full confidence that God would allow us to have twelve students. Before long, I realized how little faith I had. I had once again underestimated what God could do. Twenty pastors-students showed up all at once, almost double what we'd prayed for. But then more and more people streamed in until the place became absolutely chaotic! Pastor Paul's house could not accommodate the *145* attendees who showed up. We had to move our operation out onto the street.

So began LIT Cuba. And the Lord provided all the finances we needed. God sent many unexpected gifts at the most opportune times. One time a Baptist megachurch in Houston sent a check for $35,000 with an additional $25,000 each subsequent year, because they believed in what we were doing in Cuba. Another time one of LIT's ESL instructors, Jerry White, walked into my office, holding two gold bars. The church he had been a member of decided to close down and prayerfully sought ways to disburse their assets. Jerry had told them about what New Life had been doing in Cuba and the pastor agreed to give us their two ten-ounce gold bars.

Many churches and individual Christians all over the world sent regular and lump-sum offerings, which allowed us to expand our ministry in Cuba. I still marvel at the miraculous works of God in that country.

Chapter Thirty-Three

———•———

UNIVIDA

A FEW MONTHS BEFORE WE LAUNCHED LIT, a tall and handsome man walked into my Houston church office and introduced himself as Tony Perez from Camaguey, Cuba. He was visiting the United States and had gotten my name from a pastor in Havana. He seemed very confident for a young man and shared his vision for campus ministry in Cuba. He had worked with a few leaders to conduct small Bible studies but he lamented that there was a lack of network and financial backing for the ministry to grow. His passion glowed as he talked about the unlimited potential of this ministry with the right kind of leadership and organization.

This piqued my interest, because I had always wanted to be involved in campus ministry. My head swelled with questions: Is God opening another door besides LIT Cuba? Am I greedy to take on more responsibilities? Am I spreading myself too thin by venturing into something new?

I determined to spend more time in prayer and study to discern God's *mahashaba* on this. Truth be told, I had difficulty praying because my heart was eager to dive into this ministry and my mind was sold out to getting involved.

When Tony went back to Cuba, I had him organize a retreat in the city of Morón for about 200 college students. Most of them were from the Camaguey region, one of the largest provinces in central Cuba, about 350 miles southeast of Havana. We bused them all to the northwest corner of the region in Morón, where we found a Methodist pastor who was willing to work with us and let us use his church facility. I raised enough funds to finance the total cost of the students' food, lodging, and transportation. We held seminars and workshops during the day and revival meetings open to the public in the evenings. Each afternoon I challenged the students to pair up, knock on every household door in the adjacent area, and witness about Jesus or invite them to the evening service. At that time, the Cuban government was not cracking down on the Cubans witnessing to other Cubans, but it did not tolerate foreigners like me going outside the church with the message of the gospel.

With the end of the retreat, I returned to Houston

only to be visited by Tony again a few months later. He stopped by my office to tell me that he had decided to stay in America and would bring his family also when it was legally possible. He asked if he could work under me in the church and be discipled. His goal was to become an ordained minister.

I couldn't make this decision on my own, so I brought it before the deacons. They were impressed with this young man's desire to serve the Lord, so they decided to sponsor his visa and help him settle in Houston. I also made arrangements with the Baptist General Convention of Texas to help him plant a Hispanic church within our congregation. He started with a few Cuban immigrants, and the church grew to about thirty strong. In about a year and half, Tony brought his wife and daughter to Houston.

In the meantime, I flew back and forth to Cuba to work with Freddie Borquez, another young man Tony had introduced to me. Freddie had made arrangements for us to meet with the Christian student leaders of the University of Havana, with the purpose of establishing a campus ministry.

Freddie and I waited along the Malecón in front of the monument of USS *Maine*, which was erected in 1925 in honor of US sailors who died in 1898 during the Spanish-American War. Freddie and I waited for an hour in the cold, windy, damp evening before we began to worry that something had happened to the leaders. Or possibly they sensed someone was following them and decided not to show up for our own safety. We scanned the area for any suspicious activity but found none. It began to feel like a scene out of Syndey Pollack's movie *Havana*.

Freddie called one of the men we were to meet. After several more calls, he rescheduled and moved the meeting to a fast-food restaurant, where it was more crowded and, therefore, safer. When we arrived, I spotted a group of six intelligent-looking men and women. They were all business.

Their blunt and unexpected question stunned me: "What makes you different from others who have proposed something similar? Why should we trust you?"

"Who are these 'others'?" I said.

One man spoke up. "Some years before, a group of Canadians representing Campus Crusade for Christ visited. They conducted several meetings with the Christian leaders from the university—some of us included—and explained about their work and resources to grow the campus ministry. They left with a promise that they would return shortly. The students were exuberant at the prospect of the campus ministry and eagerly awaited CCC's return.

"A few months later, they did return but were

detained at the airport for bringing a slew of teaching materials with them. The officials interrogated them for hours, and, in the end, they deported the CCC members back to Canada. Evidently this scared them so much, they dropped all contact with us. It was like they evaporated.

"Other groups have come from the United States, but like CCC, they talked big and then they left. So, again I ask, what makes you different?"

I understood their skepticism, but I knew my heart. "I did not come to Cuba to make promises. I do not have a large church or a lot of money to bring to you. But I am simply following the Lord and want to serve Him. I believe He has led me here. In obedience to Him, I have started a Bible institute in Havana, and if He opens an opportunity for campus ministry, I will follow His directions. I don't want to say anything to give you false hope, nor do I want to persuade you into working with me. I think I can help you—exactly how, I don't know, but I'm certain the Lord will show me."

And then I shared with them my experience in working with young people in the United States, along with my vision for such a ministry in Cuba. "Pockets of ministries have popped up in some provincial universities, but no organized national ministry or network exists. This presents a golden opportunity to start an organization that would unify these ministries scattered across the country. I see the potential for some sort of connection between the campus ministry and LIT Cuba. Perhaps some college students have callings in their lives to be trained in LIT and become church planters."

When I finished, the leaders gave no response. An uncomfortable silence hung between us. Then one after another, they seemed to soften. I perceived a slight shift in their perspective. We came to no solid conclusions; however, we parted by agreeing to pray about the matter and meet again.

Freddie immediately started to establish a network of existing campus ministries among the Cuban universities. Though the other university ministries quickly joined the network, the leaders from the University of Havana were reticent—I'm sure because of previous experiences. But after more than a year of observing that we were here to stay, they joined our network. Two other provincial universities in the east that had been meeting on their own also came on board with us.

The next question was, what would we call our campus ministry? I left it up to Freddie and the leaders. After much thought and discussion they came up with *Univida* (*Universidad Vida*), which means "university life." In just a few months—July 2002—*Univida* would hold its first retreat in Cespedes, roughly 350 miles southeast of Havana.

Chapter Thirty-Four

—◦—

KEY STRATEGY

ONE OF OUR MOST MEMORABLE MOMENTS was March 5, 2004, when we graduated the first class of LIT Cuba: seventy-four students. (Almost half of the original 145 students dropped out because of various difficulties, such as transportation problems and family issues.)

We rented a relatively large church in which to hold the graduation ceremony. Several deacons from Houston accompanied me on that trip. I delivered a message challenging the graduates to go and make disciples of all nations. The battle was about to begin, so fight the good fight, run the course, and keep your faith, as Paul exhorted Timothy (2 Tim. 4:7). And then I laid my hands on the top ten graduates, whom we commissioned to go out and find communities that had no churches, and challenged them to plant churches.

We instituted this commissioning because

while traveling throughout Cuba, I had noticed that most of the churches were concentrated in heavily populated areas, but many rural areas lacked churches. One summer, I was traveling with a team from New Life through the province of Guantanamo. The van we had rented broke down in a mountainous area, and we had to walk two miles to get to the nearest phone to call for help.

Knowing it would take several hours for help to arrive, I challenged the team members to form into pairs, witness to the villagers, and visit the remote farmhouses on the horizon. They were understandably hesitant and some even complained that they did not speak the language. And on top of that, the weather was stifling. I reminded them that language does not save people; rather, it's the work of the Spirit. I encouraged them to use sign language if necessary, and then I almost forcefully dispatched them.

In a few hours, the teams started making their way back. I had to laugh because even from a distance, I could see the joy in their smiling faces. And better yet, they were not returning alone. Along with them were many to whom they had witnessed. Every team had a story to tell, and they did so with excitement. They were incredulous how God could use them in leading these farmers to accept the Lord and attain salvation. Many of the villagers brought sacks of coconuts and other fruits out of gratitude.

In an effort to make sure of their understanding, I used an interpreter to explain the gospel and what their decisions for the Lord meant. Once I was satisfied they understood, I encouraged them to get involved in a local church to keep their faith growing. That's when the smiles faded and they stared at me with stunned expressions.

"Where is the closest church?" I asked.

"It's over thirty miles from here, toward Guantanamo City."

Now it was my turn to be stunned. Then it became a moment of enlightenment. We can preach the gospel all we want, but if we don't have churches to disciple believers in these areas, our efforts could be in vain. As I later discovered, hundreds of places like this all across the country are without churches. This was when I considered it our mission to plant churches in the areas where no churches exist within a five-mile radius. This was the turning point in our ministry.

We often misinterpret the Great Commission by placing too heavy an emphasis on spreading the gospel and leading people to Christ. While this is certainly the core of our message in any kind of missionary work, the key words are "make disciples." To fulfill this requires more than getting a person saved and then moving on to the next, or introducing the townspeople to Jesus and then going to the next city. We need look no further than the book of Acts and study Paul's three-part strategy. Without exception, he witnessed the gospel, made disciples, and planted churches. Therefore, this is our example to follow.

Another reason for planting local churches is to bring a transformation to the community itself.

One of our first graduates, Janet, told me the story of how she and her husband established the church in Amarillas.

One day she wandered the rural area outside of Havana, asking God to show her what He wanted her to do. She discovered the village of Amarillas, which had no church. She desired to plant a church there, but she lived in Havana, a two-hour drive from the village—if she had a car.

Janet had two options: hitchhike to and from Amarillas, or move to the village and become a part of the community. We Americans can move from one city to another if we desire. We can just as easily move from state to state. But in Cuba it's not so simple. To relocate, Janet would first have to apply with the government for a vacancy of an apartment in Amarillas. Vacancies are hard to come by.

Janet and her husband, Eliezer, who had graduated a year after she did, made several trips to Amarillas. They scouted the area, and as they walked the village, they prayed for God to act upon the land. One day, they noticed some children playing in the street. Janet and Eliezer decided they would start their outreach with them.

Every time they visited Amarillas, Eliezer played his guitar and Janet sang while using hand and dance motions, which immediately attracted the kids. Then it didn't take long for a crowd to form around Janet, Eliezer, and the children. The children's young mothers were among the spectators. Most of the girls in Amarillas gave birth to their children at around age fifteen or sixteen, and several of these mothers were pregnant with their second and third children.

After several songs, Janet told stories from the Bible and eventually talked about Jesus Christ. One by one the mothers accepted the Lord, and in a few months, a church was planted in a believer's backyard behind a farmhouse, where the pigs and goats competed for space.

The Amarillas church developed a Sunday school for the children, and their young mothers brought their husbands and parents. The church formed organically, and people were genuinely happy to gather and praise God.

One story Janet told was especially moving. One of the notorious villagers was a seventy-two-year-old man, José. His best and only "friend" was alcohol. He wandered the streets, swearing and cussing at the top of his voice while in his drunken stupor. Mothers grabbed their children and hustled them inside if this foul-mouthed village nuisance ventured down their street. Everyone avoided him.

As the worshippers gathered for their evening service one Sunday, mosquitoes and moths buzzed and fluttered around the lone light bulb hanging from a single line hot-wired from the farmhouse. Neighborhood dogs dozed during the congregation's passionate singing. On this night, the old drunk sneaked into the backyard church and stood outside the puddle of the feeble light.

José listened as Janet spoke about the Lord. She told Bible stories as if they'd really happened and were more than just tales of make-believe characters. She spoke about Jesus as if He were a man she personally knew.

That night, when Eliezer gave the invitation while playing his guitar, the old man stepped forward. Tears streamed down his cheeks. They were good tears that brought a cleansing deep within him. That night he became a free man. He rid himself of all the things that had bound him for so many years—alcohol, tobacco, and anger.

He was a poet of sort, although no one had acknowledged his gift. He improvised spiritual poems about his feelings. When I had the honor of baptizing him a few months after his Sunday night conversion, he recited a poem that expressed his experience. He became a hungry student of the Word. As he studied the Scriptures, he became convicted that he and his common-law wife had lived together for many years without being officially married. In fact, few people in this town cared much about weddings, mostly because they couldn't afford the license fees or even a modest celebration. José asked Eliezer and Janet to officiate their wedding. Janet took this as another opportunity to witness to the folks.

Many of the villagers came out of curiosity, as they had never attended a wedding. They were thoroughly impressed because Janet and Eliezer made it beautiful and fun and inexpensive. Shortly thereafter, droves of young couples lined up to be married in the presence of God. As a result, many became Christians. Thus began Amarillas's transformation.

One resident was not so thrilled with the changes in the hearts of the people. A Santería priest had been a dominant spiritual force in that town. Santería is a common religion in Cuba that mixes African and Caribbean pagan worship with Catholicism. Practices include animal sacrifices and communication with the dead. It is rumored, and most Cubans believe, that Fidel Castro is a follower of Santería. Raul, Fidel's brother and current president of Cuba, is also said to be a Santería follower.

This religion is flat-out demonic. Most of the rural areas are heavily influenced by this practice. I have encountered many Cubans who are demonically possessed because of the exposure to the pagan rituals performed by the priests. Rituals commonly involve the use of rooster or other animal blood. A major component of the religion includes going into trances and frenzies. Of course, followers of Santería are discouraged from associating with Christians, and priests will perform rituals to disrupt the churches. They are not necessarily violent in their opposition; however, the religion poses a spiritual battle for the churches and Christians.

However, God is not hindered by Satan's purveyors of deceit and fear. Emboldened by the Holy Spirit, Janet and Eliezer witnessed to this Santería priest. Though he lived with his wife in a spooky house deep within the woods, Janet and Eliezer persisted with their outreach to his family.

And then it happened. The power and love of the Holy Spirit overwhelmed the priest and his wife. They accepted Christ as their Savior and Lord and renounced Santería. The former priest had a barn full of idols, and he didn't hesitate to burn all of them when he became a free man in the Lord. He didn't stop there. He began to witness to his followers to abandon witchcraft and seek the truth in Jesus, and many did.

One of my friends, Don Bryan, was so moved by Janet and Eliezer's work that he gave me money to buy them a house in Amarillas. Their home doubled as the church. But their congregation quickly outgrew the house, so Janet planted two more churches in the same town. This couple's dedication and commitment transformed the whole town that had been gripped by the forces of darkness for so many years.

Within the first year of the harvest from LIT Cuba (2004), we planted ten community churches across the country. I knew then what direction God wanted us to follow with this ministry.

Chapter Thirty-Five

THE CHALLENGE

IN THE SUMMER OF 2004, I TOOK A GROUP of college students from New Life to Cuba. I was to lead a seminar for the pastors in Havana. New Life Church in Houston paid all the expenses for the Cuban pastors attending the seminar, including food and transportation.

One of my group leaders pulled me aside before the seminar commenced and reported that she suspected Pastor Paul, the director of LIT Cuba, might be pocketing some of the money I had given him to buy food for the attendees. *No way,* I thought. *Not Pastor Paul.* I reprimanded her for thinking such a thing as well as accusing this fine man without presenting specific proof. For the moment, I rejected her accusations. But I would soon discover I should have paid attention.

I was always privileged to have Yarine at my side as

my personal translator each time I went to Cuba. He was among our first graduates of LIT and, amazingly, was one of the top interpreters working for Fidel Castro. It was common to see him on the front pages of *Granma* alongside dignitaries visiting Fidel.

When questioned by the Communist bosses about his refusal to join the party, Yarine boldly told them that he was Christian. This was his personal decision, but it did not mean he was any less patriotic or loyal to his beloved country, nor would it conflict with his being an interpreter. He demanded that they respect his faith, yet he told them he understood if they felt they needed to let him go. This put the party officials in a predicament, because his translation skill was one of the best, and he had proven his commitment and trustworthiness time and again. He had even spent a year in New York as translator for the Cuban delegation to the United Nations. The party leaders could not agree to dismiss him, yet his refusal to join the Communist party meant he would never receive any promotions.

A man of deep faith, Yarine was in his thirties. Just like Joseph in the Bible, he had seen future events in his dreams. When we first met, he claimed that he had already seen me in a dream. He said that the Lord showed him what I looked like and even that I was coming from Texas. Incredibly, he prophesied that we would be working together side by side, teaching workers and planting churches.

On the last evening of the seminar and the night before I would be leaving Cuba, Yarine called and said he and two others wanted to see me about an important matter. It was getting late and I was almost ready to go to bed, but I agreed to see them if they came to the place where I was staying.

Yarine arrived with two instructors for LIT Cuba, Ariel and Noel, both of whom were in their late twenties. They were concerned about the management of the school, and it had mostly to do with Pastor Paul. They were certain he was embezzling LIT funds, as well as double-dealing with another church in Alabama by basically doing the same thing for them as for us. He was also rumored to be carrying on an affair with the school's secretary.

But even beyond all of this, they claimed he was teaching some unorthodox doctrines in the school. One such teaching he pushed was that the gift of tongues was evidence of salvation. In addition, he loosely interpreted the gift of prophecy as more like foretelling the future and one's fortune rather than its biblical meaning. He taught and spoke of his own experiences and testimonies as being more important than following the Bible.

I could hardly believe that Paul would be involved in such blatant sin and error. I tried to appeal to my visitors for patience and more prayer, encouraging them that God would eventually prevail.

But to my surprise, they said they could no longer work in the school, even though they'd have to give up their monthly $25 stipend. While that's pocket money to US citizens, giving it up would be a major sacrifice for their families. But they were firm that this was the right thing to do, because they had to follow their consciences. They believed God would honor them for their stand. They would not be associated with this ungodly man.

I was at first devastated, but as I allowed the truth to sink in, I could see where the Lord was leading. Was He cleansing our ministry before taking us to the next level?

I asked the young men to give me a month to reflect on the situation, pray about it, and make a decision. I was grateful that they agreed to this. Then I asked who they thought was best qualified to replace Paul. Both Yarine and Noel said it was undoubtedly Ariel Cruz.

We went to our knees in heartfelt prayer. We held hands and poured out our hearts for the future of Cuba as the summer breeze flowed over us, cooling our faces.

Chapter Thirty-Six

——•——

CHANGE

MAKING CHANGES, ESPECIALLY IN personnel, is never easy but many times necessary.

I made another trip to Cuba in September 2004, after a lot of thought and prayer. At Ariel's recommendation, I first visited with Pastor Alejandro Nieto, the senior pastor of Liga Evangélica, a large church in Havana, about the possibility of moving our LIT Cuba school to his church. He was also the overseer of approximately 250 churches he had helped establish all across Cuba.

Alejandro's father had planted Liga Evangélica with the help of an American missionary who ministered in Cuba some years before Castro came to power. With the revolution and the successful overthrow of the Cuban government, the missionary was forced to return to America. The church, however, continued to grow, even under intense persecution. The members were forced to meet in homes to avoid scrutiny by the authorities, thus giving rise to the house-church movement.

Alejandro was a young man in his twenties when his father went to be with the Lord, and he was suddenly thrown into the leadership position. The church leaders had many doubts the church could survive, much less mature and grow, under such an inexperienced and young leader. But Alejandro proved them wrong. He turned out to be a dynamic and ambitious leader, and the church expanded under his leadership much more than it did with his father's.

As I sat across from Alejandro, he impressed me not only with his kindness but also with his strong personality and fluent English.

Without hesitation, he welcomed our school but added a stipulation. "One thing I want to ask of you is not to bring any pollution here."

"Pardon? What do you mean by 'pollution'?"

"I have known Paul for many years. He and I risked our lives working for the Lord in the seventies and eighties. I believe he is basically a good man, but over the years money has smeared his vision. I am afraid he has yielded to material things. As you may have noticed in my country, it is very difficult to stay focused on the ministry without worrying about where your family's next meal will come from. Even pastors get worn out and give in to temptation. Wherever they find the easy money, there they will go. This is what has happened to Paul. This is spiritual pollution we don't want in our church. If you want to move here, don't bring any baggage that belongs to him."

So even Alejandro was aware of Paul's dealings. I dislike confrontation and try to avoid it, but I had to do the right thing for the school, and, of course, Matthew 18 gives a mandate about steps to take with a brother in Christ caught in sin. So I left Alejandro and immediately went to Paul's house.

I first pointed out his wrongdoings. He denied everything and turned cool toward me. He rejected any correction and, thus, any opportunity to reconcile the situation. Even after I presented him with proof, Paul refused to acknowledge any misconduct; therefore, I had no choice but to relieve him of his job and all association with the school.

The ensuing violent screaming match that erupted, in which his wife and daughters joined, blindsided me. I had never encountered such a situation—and I pray I never do again. Not only would he not relinquish the equipment, books, supplies, and student records that belonged to the school, he swore he'd turn the school's staff and students against me. He made good on his promise, sadly. In the end we lost most of the equipment as well as the students and even some of the instructors. I now understood Pastor Alejandro's warning about "pollution."

After an event such as this, it's natural to look back and wonder how the situation deteriorated so badly. I have to confess that my confidence in administering LIT, as well as other arms of ministry, was sorely shaken. Surely there had been signs that something was wrong with Paul, so how did I miss them? Looking back I realized I hadn't missed them, but they didn't register as red flags. Every time I returned to Cuba and visited Paul, I noticed something new in his home—a TV, DVD player, furniture, new cell phone, etc. What happened to my discernment?

Then I began questioning if I should have confronted Paul and "fired" him. Maybe I should have been more lenient or tried to work with him. Though I offered a continued relationship, Paul rejected it and instead chose to be antagonistic. But I had to look at the facts: one member noticed Paul's cheating, three instructors knew of his embezzlement and false teaching, Pastor Alejandro's awareness of Paul's dealings and called it pollution.

At times I felt I might have made a big mistake in the way I handled Paul, for the future of LIT looked grim. But I chose to take the situation and the facts to prayer. I gave God my questions about my own ability and even the ministry itself. I cast all these cares on Him, knowing I would receive from Him truth and clarity. If this ministry was from Him, then He would reestablish the vision.

Emerging from these times of searching prayer, I became confident that the school was a good work from the Lord, and ousting Paul was the right thing to do, hard as it was. If I had continued with Paul, my later regrets would have been a huge cost to pay. In some ways, confronting Paul was reminiscent of my confrontation with Pearl S. Buck many years before. I wanted to do the right thing, regardless of the personal cost. It was unpleasant, but at least I don't have to live with haunting what-ifs. I did what was right, learned a few lessons, and moved on.

Basically we had to start from scratch to rebuild the LIT Cuba ministry. It was a slow process in the beginning, but Ariel was steadfast in his commitment to hard work, and our first students came from within Alejandro's church.

New Life's deacon Yong Lee donated enough funds to buy ten computers and printers. Now we could set up a computer lab so the school could offer computer courses. Though you and I can go to any number of stores or even shop online for computers, in those days Cubans were not allowed to buy computers. Even if a Cuban had special permission from the government to buy one, he or she could not purchase in bulk.

But the Cubans find ways to make things work. A good example is their cars. A typical '56 Chevy may have a Russian engine, Peugeot transmission, and other homemade parts. Many such ingeniously "mixed" cars are on the road today in Cuba.

So we had the funds for ten sets of computers and printers, but how would we buy them?

Yarine had a way. He worked with many embassies, which are exempt from import regulations and are free to shop from the government stores without many restrictions. He knew the staff at the Equatorial Guinea Embassy and arranged for them to make the purchase for us. Of course, they'd require a 15 percent "handling fee."

The computers were a huge hit with the students. Enrollment dramatically increased. Part of our curriculum is a three-day seminar in a retreat setting prior to graduation. There we train the students on the principles and practical methodology of the church-planting movement.

Two years after re-opening our doors in Pastor Alejandro's church, LIT Cuba graduated over 250 students. Twenty of these we commissioned to plant churches in remote areas. The new LIT school was sending its roots down deep in Cuba.

Chapter Thirty-Seven

---•---

THE MOVE

IN 2006 THE DEACON BOARD AT NEW LIFE sought God's guidance in relocating the church. We had outgrown our facility and concluded that the place was not suitable in reaching the vision God had given to us. In addition, the building did not meet the current city codes to continue to function as a church and a school. We also felt we were throwing money out the window by paying the high rent.

But we were in a quandary because we had no building fund. We decided to search for a location and see if God would provide the funds, or at least show us which direction we were to go. We knew this kind of venture would be a long-term process.

One day I stumbled upon a Baptist church close to my house in Sugar Land. It was for sale for $2.5 million. The amount was beyond our reach, so the possibility would not have been on my plate for consideration, but my curiosity and the fact that it was along my normal driving pattern propelled me to investigate it. Its sheer size impressed me. The property included seven acres of land alongside a major toll road. It also had two buildings: a one-story sanctuary and a two-story Sunday school building. Although the parking lot was in need of repair, it had enough space for over a hundred cars.

I really liked the complex. It possessed so much potential. But I had to return to reality because New Life had no money for this pie-in-the-sky dream.

Just as I was about to turn my car around to leave the parking lot, a woman came out of the church office. She must have noticed me, because she flagged me down. I just wanted to leave, but I didn't want to be rude.

"I was just admiring your buildings but was about to leave. My church is in the market for a building, but we don't have any money."

"Our pastor is in his office, and he would be happy to see you. Why don't you come in and just chat with him awhile?" she said—insisted.

I reluctantly went in and met with Sam Waltman. He settled into his office chair and shared how the church had arrived where they were. "The church had been a predominantly white church since its inception, but because of the demographic changes in the area, many of the members have moved farther away. I'm sure you know that West Oaks was once considered one of the desirable suburban communities on the west side of Houston, but now the suburbs have moved even farther west. As a result, we're having severe financial problems. So we've decided to close it down and transfer the liquid assets to another Baptist church. The real estate market is sluggish, so we're looking for any reasonable offer."

I shared with Pastor Sam a little about New Life and our ministry in Cuba, which particularly seemed to impress him.

"Why don't you put together a proposal and make an offer? I'll present it to my board."

I informed the leaders of New Life of my visit with this pastor and his suggestion. They thought it best to invest lots of time in prayer before making any kind of decision. We prayed together and individually. We had to discern God's plan.

After several days, we came together to compare our spiritual notes. The consensus was that we would offer $1.2 million, a little less than half of the asking price. It was quickly accepted by West Oaks Baptist Church. I immediately appealed to the congregation to donate as much and as quickly as they could. We collected $350,000. I arranged financing for the balance and hired David Smith, an attorney friend who was also my client when I was in banking, to handle the legalities and the title search.

As we were getting close to closing, David called me. "There's a problem with the deed and title policy. It's a big problem."

"Will it keep us from buying this property?"

"Actually, it might be a blessing to you. When the land was originally purchased in partnership with Westbury and River Oaks Baptist churches many years before, they put in the deed a stipulation that it was to be used only for the purpose of church. They had a vision that Houston was expanding west and that they would plant a mission on the property someday, so they felt it necessary to lock up the land for a specific purpose. This is great for New Life because you are a church and likely wouldn't use it for any other purpose. But from a legal and business perspective, this stipulation devalues the land."

"I'm still not sure what the problem is, Dave."

"Get the property reappraised and then based on that, revise your offer. As it stands, the property has zero commercial value. You could not sell it if Walmart or Walgreens made an offer—no matter how enticing."

When I broke this news to Sam, he expressed his desire to keep the deal alive somehow. He again encouraged the deacons and me to come up with our best offer.

The deacons were divided. One group saw this as a blessing from the Lord and an opportunity to buy it with the cash we had on hand, thus not going into debt. The other group also thought this was the work of God to bless us, but that we should not try to steal it. We should make a reasonable offer of what it was worth. Again we waited until the Spirit united our thinking. We unanimously concluded that a $720,000 offer was reasonable under the circumstances. The seller accepted without countering.

Chapter Thirty-Eight

---•---

DEPORTATION REVISITED

MARCH 2008 MARKED MY THIRTY-FIFTH trip to Cuba. As I normally had done since we obtained the travel license from the Treasury Department, I was flying out of Miami via a chartered flight. These flights were used by Cuban Americans who were allowed to visit their relatives once every two years, and they were convenient for those of us with the license to piggyback on them.

When I landed in Havana, a surprise was waiting for me. The immigration officer took away my passport and ordered me to wait in the lobby. Relegated to the empty lobby, I feverishly tried to figure out what had caused my current situation. I hadn't done anything illegal. My travel license was up-to-date. Had some governmental snafu taken place that I was unaware of?

A couple of uniformed military officers chit-chatted across the room but obviously couldn't care less about helping me by explaining what was going on.

Finally, after I'd waited and worried for about two hours, the officer returned. She handed me my passport, and in broken English said I must go back to Miami. I was flabbergasted and demanded to know why.

She simply shrugged. "You leave. Return to Miami and don't come back!"

I kept asking the reason for this, but I made no headway. So I asked her how long before I could return.

She shrugged again, which infuriated me.

I wanted to help her answer my question, so I said, "Never?"

"Yes."

To this date I still do not know whether she understood my question or answered just to shut me up. But I had no choice but to remain in the airport for the next charter flight back to Miami. My wait seemed eternal before one finally arrived. After the arriving passengers deplaned, a couple of Cuban soldiers with rifles slung on their shoulders escorted me to the plane, put me in the backseat, and made sure I was securely buckled in.

Flying back to Miami, I tried to process what had happened and why. I checked into the Hilton at the airport, and as soon as I dropped my suitcase on the floor, I knelt by the bed. "Lord, you know I don't mind suffering for You. In fact, it will be an honor. But why is this happening now? We are just getting organized in Cuba, and the timing couldn't be worse. How can the work go on without me there? Lord, I don't understand. Please help make sense out of this madness!"

I broke down and cried. It seemed an end had arrived to our ministry in Cuba. I fell asleep while still kneeling on the carpeted floor.

And then a whisper woke me up.

Trust Me, My son, for I have a plan for you, a plan to prosper you and not harm you, a plan to give you hope and future. Can you trust Me?

It was the familiar voice of the Lord. I knew it because He spoke to me the same way when He gave me the vision of planting 100 churches, supporting 1,000 missionaries, making 10,000 disciples, and introducing 100,000 souls to Christ.

"Yes, Lord, I trust You." Though I reluctantly showed my displeasure of what had just happened.

When we believe in something strongly, we do not like anything to change the course or get in the way. But notice the word *something* and not *Someone*. Sometimes we get carried away in the work, or the *something*, so that we tend to forget for Whom we are working. Psalm 37:23 says, "The LORD makes firm the steps of the one who delights in him." George Müller, the great evangelist from the 1800s and director of Ashley Down orphanage in Bristol, England, wrote in the margin of his Bible next to that psalm: "The Lord is sovereign and orders the steps and stops."

Whatever the reason, this was the stop the Lord was ordering. Despite my intense dislike, I had to submit.

Chapter Thirty-Nine

THE DESERT

FOR REASONS YET UNEXPLAINED TO ME, I was unable to go to Cuba for three long years. Still, the work there continued to flourish—even more so than when I was able to go. Sue and some members organized trips and attended graduations of LIT Cuba on my behalf. Ariel continued his hard work, and obviously the Lord was blessing us despite my not being able to visit, which to me felt like some kind of hidden opposition. Just thinking about those workers and students broke my heart. The positive news about the continued harvest gave me a tremendous amount of courage.

In the meantime, I wanted to pursue another vision I'd always had: North Korea. Both of Sue's parents had been born in North Korea, and on numerous occasions they had asked me to promise to plant a church in their hometown. I did promise that I would do my best, but, of course, God would have to remove the obstacles and give us an opening. For years I prayed and encouraged my congregation to pray that we would have a way to take the gospel into North Korea. As of yet, nothing seemed to be happening.

One day I decided to visit as near to the North Korean border as I could. So I asked God to show me a place in China where we could start our ministry, and whether it involved establishing a school or something else. I was open to His direction.

So I first flew to Beijing then on to Shenyang. From there I took a bus to Dandong, a city closest to the northwest border of North Korea. The Yalu River, a huge body of water, divides the two countries. A bridge spanned the river at one time. It was partially destroyed during the Korean War, and a remnant of it is still intact halfway over the water. This is where General MacArthur wanted to advance into China, but as a result of his statements contrary to the White House's policy, President Truman relieved him of duty.

As I rode the tourist ferry that took us almost within a stone's throw of the North Korean border, I observed several Koreans. Some rode antiquated bicycles and others just squatted and smoked. A few made obscene gestures, and one fellow even threw a rock at us. In the distance, I spotted several rust-covered factories or warehouses that looked as if they were either idle or had fallen into severe disrepair.

Lord, open the door for us so we can tell them about Your Son.

I had to cut my trip short because a popular Christian TV station in Seoul, South Korea, wanted to tape an interview with me about our work in Cuba. After the interview, I flew back to Beijing to spend my last night there before heading home. I had an address and phone number of Timothy Lee, a Korean missionary I had known for some years. I called him and invited him to have dinner with me.

Timothy had been struggling to keep his small congregation going in the outskirts of Beijing. He prayed for fresh direction from the Lord. I shared with him about the possibility of starting a Learning Institute of Texas in China to train workers for witnessing to the North Koreans. He filled me in on the kind of information I would need about China if I were to begin a ministry there.

He cautioned me about the risks of pursuing mission opportunities in North Korea using an ESL school. Several other entities had attempted such efforts. But the only thing they had succeeded in doing was making corrupt North Korean officials richer. The common trick, which many naïve Christian businessmen have fallen for, is for a free government land lease that entices a school or a business to come into the country and pour money into getting set up. The officials usually start by requiring minimal standards, which makes the offer attractive. But the standards are fluid at best, and these officials use them to their advantage. Once they have you on the hook, they keep demanding more and more. Eventually, they confiscate your assets or close you down and push you out of North Korea.

Timothy assured me that it was virtually impossible to witness Jesus in that country without risking your life. Therefore, we needed to come up with a unique strategy to protect our interests and figure out ways to witness Christ without endangering lives. That sounded like a tall order, but nothing is too difficult for God.

We parted ways well past two o'clock in the morning, after a long and heartfelt prayer. We agreed to pursue the legal establishment of LIT China in Beijing.

Chapter Forty

---◆---

THE RETURN

It had been three years since I was refused entrance into Cuba. My desire to go back and see the leaders and the church planters was becoming so intense that I often dreamed of being there. I prayed incessantly and, frankly, grew frustrated with God's silence about the matter. And yet God is still so merciful that He even covered my audacity.

In February of 2011, I received an e-mail from Jared, whom I'd met some years before in Santa Clara, Cuba. He was originally from Holland and was working with Bill Wilson's church in New York. A young man in his twenties, he was so committed to children's ministry that he used his Dutch citizenship to apply for a student visa and attended a college in Santa Clara. This allowed him a cover to continue his ministry. But his landlord became suspicious of his activities and reported him to the authorities. They tapped his phone and after a long interrogation, they deported him to the United States. By this time, it had also been three years since his deportation from Cuba. He planned to enter Cuba via Mexico as a tourist in March and encouraged me to try the same.

I was excited at the prospect and immediately booked a flight to Cancun, Mexico. On arrival at the Cancun airport, I bought the tourist card that I hoped would get me into Cuba. I boarded the Cubana de Aviacion flight to Havana. When I landed at the José Martí International Airport in Havana and stood in the long line to go through the immigration booth, I kept praying for God's favor. "Lord, You know my heart. Please, let me go through this so I will be able to continue Your work in this country."

And then I noticed an obvious plainclothesman scanning the crowd of mostly tourists from Canada and Europe. On spotting me, he strode to me and demanded to see my passport. Thumbing through the pages, he asked the reason for my visit.

I thought this an odd question, because immigration officers normally do this kind of questioning. Although he wore no uniform or insignia, he carried a walkie-talkie; therefore, I assumed he was with the security detail. Security officers in Cuba carry absolute authority and control the masses.

What was even stranger was that he kept staring

at me as though he suspected me of something. It made me feel extremely uncomfortable, but I stared back as I told myself I had no reason to feel worried or embarrassed. He handed back my passport and motioned me to the immigration booth. This shook me up. And I was bothered that I felt so fearful. I didn't know where this fear was coming from. *In the name of Jesus, I bind the spirit of fear; you shall leave me. I command you! Lord Jesus, I am here to represent You. I am here to proclaim Your name. Please, help me!*

As I was standing in front of the immigration officer, I felt calmer and answered his questions with confidence. And then after scanning my passport, he took his time reading something on his computer screen. He told me to wait, and he left his booth to consult with someone I figured to be his superior. This was not a good sign. I knew there was a problem. I presumed that I was going to be sent back again.

When he returned momentarily, I held my breath.

"Have a nice stay in Cuba, sir."

No grass grew under my feet. I rushed out of there rejoicing!

I had a tearful reunion with my fellow partners: Ariel and his wife and two regional directors of LIT Cuba, who had been waiting patiently outside the airport.

Ariel cautioned me to be careful with my

movements, because he was certain the government was watching me. We decided it would be best for me to stay put in the *renta* (a privately-owned, rented room, similar to a bed-and-breakfast) and conduct our meetings there. On several previous occasions, I'd had agents tailing me. They'd wait outside where I was staying then follow me wherever I went. Ariel's logic was if they didn't see me leaving the house, they would get tired and give up on me.

So I stayed inside the house the three days I was in Havana, though I couldn't help but go out for a walk along Fifth Avenue (*Quinta Avenida*). The street is one of my favorite places in Havana. It is vastly different from all the other streets and areas I've visited in Cuba's capitol. Rather than bordered with dirty, ramshackle buildings, Fifth Avenue boasts architectural beauty of the embassies and the long-standing buildings dating back to the Spanish colonial days. Potholes are nonexistent. It's broad enough for people to jog, roller-skate, or simply walk. The way is lined with shrubs, flowers, and picnic benches, which give it a park-like image for several miles.

I went for long walks, sometimes taking an hour or two, resting on the benches and watching the people. After being absent from Cuba for so long, I couldn't help but thank God for allowing me the honor of my calling to minister to the Cuban people. As each person strolled, jogged, or skated by, they seemed ever so precious to me. Oh, how God values the Cuban people! I love the people in this country. I thanked God for letting me come back to Cuba.

Fortunately, I did not see any sign of anyone following me.

Several leaders came to me for prayer, and we held strategic meetings in the *renta*. I also taught them the principles of church planting by leading them in a study of several biblical models. We studied the Antioch church model in particular, the church that sent out the apostle Paul on his first missionary journey. We reviewed every word contained in the Commission: "Go and make disciples of all nations, baptizing them in the name of the Father and of the Son and of the Holy Spirit, and teaching them to obey everything I have commanded you."

"All nations" in Greek is *pas ethnos,* which literally means "all people groups" or "all ethnic groups." Although this command was given first to the disciples and the first church in Jerusalem, it was not carried out until Stephen's martyrdom, which caused the *diaspora* and resulted in some believers ending up in Antioch. It was only when they started to reach out to *pas ethnos* that the Commission was accurately carried out.

It has been 2000 years since our Lord gave the Great Commission to the church. Although it is impossible to know the exact statistics, approximately less than 40 percent of the world's population *recognizes* the name of our Lord; therefore, the percentage of believers would be far less than that. It is startling when you compare that with what Coca-Cola has been able to accomplish. The company is barely a hundred years old, and yet over 90 percent of the world's population recognizes its name. This is the result of the clear goal-setting and aggressive marketing efforts by Coca-Cola's board of directors. They have successfully marketed their product as the "Real Thing" all over the world. In a word, Coke has far better name recognition than Jesus Christ. It is sad and tragic.

The Bible tells us that "… God exalted him to the highest place and gave him the name that is above every name, that at the name of Jesus every knee should bow, in heaven and on earth and under the earth, and every tongue confess that Jesus Christ is Lord, to the glory of God the Father" (Phil. 2:9–11). We bear the holiest, the highest, and the mightiest name. And it is the only name given to humanity that saves people from eternal hell. And that name is Jesus Christ. The name of Coke does not come even close. It is powerless to do anything.

Then who is responsible for not having reached *pas ethnos* during the past 2,000 years and making known the greatest name God has given to us?

Obviously, the churches and the Christians must bear the full blame. We must reexamine the purpose and the mission of each church and redirect our ministries. If Coca-Cola can reach *pas ethnos* in a hundred years, we must be able to do the same. After all, we have the *real* Real Thing.

I believe the answer lies in church planting. In his book *Church Planting Movements*, David Garrison defines CPM (church planting movement) as "a rapid and exponential increase of indigenous churches planting churches within a given people group or population segment." I became convinced that this was what the Lord wanted us to do. He spoke clearly to me through the Scriptures while I was teaching and reaffirmed it in my heart through the Holy Spirit. If the leaders of churches were as convinced as I was about the importance of reproducing themselves by training their people to plant churches, I believe we could evangelize the entire island nation in a relatively short time. If we could ignite the fire of this movement, we should be able to "export" this to other nations.

I taught my Cuban brothers and sisters what I believe God wanted to do in their country. Of course, the Spirit had already been at work initiating a strong movement, evidenced by the incredible number of house churches springing up in the major cities. But I noticed three things were missing, in a way very similar to the problems I identified previously with the Jerusalem church. First, this was not a movement per se; rather, it was more of a phenomenon, because I did not see any cohesive or intentional endeavor by any church or leaders. There was no centralized effort or organization, or in many cases, any connection among the underground churches.

Second is a lack of formal education. Although Cuba enjoys one of the highest literacy rates among Spanish-speaking countries (second only to Spain), many pastors barely possess a high school education. But more important, many of these house-church pastors lack a theological foundation. Without training, their messages are based on their feelings and experiences. As I mentioned earlier, the pastors have a strong desire to study systematic theology. Only a handful of seminaries are worth attending in Cuba, and the government restricts the number of enrollments the schools can accept. And then most of these leaders lack the financial ability to pay the tuition.

Third, most of the churches are focused locally and not nationally. Perhaps this can be attributed to the restraints placed on the Cubans by the government. The people have no freedom of relocation, which forces the pastors to center their efforts within their cities. Transportation difficulties also add to their struggles.

Through our strategic meetings and prayers, we

concluded that we would take our school to the cities. Ariel and the leaders traveled the length of the country and visited many pastors of established churches. We wanted to minimize the overhead by inviting the pastors with church buildings to join our ministry. We looked for places where we did not have to pay rent. At first we set up schools in five major cities.

As of this writing, we have established thirty-five LIT schools all across Cuba, with a current enrollment of over 1,000 students. We have graduated over 3,000 students and planted 185 churches in the areas where no churches are within a five-mile radius. Some of our churches are in such remote areas we can reach them only by donkey or on foot. Every Sunday over 2,500 people gather to worship the Lord, learning to invest their prayers, energy, and resources in reproducing churches.

Chapter Forty-One

———•———

ON THE HORIZON

Cuba

UNDER THE DIRECTION OF ARIEL CRUZ, the National Director of LIT Cuba, we divided the island country into six regions and appointed a director for each. Since then, Ariel has moved to Houston and serves as one of my associate pastors in charge of our Spanish ministry.

Recently, I returned to Cuba to reiterate the direction of LIT and to review our strategies and goals with the regional directors. The very essence of our ministry calls for complying with the Great Commission by presenting the gospel, baptizing believers, making disciples, and planting churches in the unchurched areas. Of course, the ultimate goal is to repeat this process throughout Cuba and beyond. LIT is a God-given instrument to carry out this mission. I made certain that all of our leaders are committed to each phase of the Great Commission.

Today we operate LIT in thirty-five locations in Cuba, seven in Mexico, and one in China. In spring of 2015, we anticipate over 1000 graduates from these schools. To be determined are the number of these graduates who will move into unchurched areas and begin new plants.

For the fifteen years we've been in Cuba, each year the enrollment in LIT increases 20 percent on average. By all counts, we foresee this trend continuing; therefore, our goal is to have planted a total of 1000 churches around the world by 2020, far surpassing my vision of planting 100 churches.

Beijing and North Korea

After many trials and errors, LIT China is finally gaining a foothold in Beijing, because we now offer English, Chinese, and Korean to both Chinese and international students. Seeing so many small and mid-sized entities forced out of China, we have meticulously followed Chinese laws and ways of doing business. We are sticking with our long-term strategy of reaching financial independence and becoming a viable business so that we will eventually be able to find a way to branch out into North Korea.

We have looked at various mission opportunities in the northeastern area of China, such as helping the refugees from North Korea, working with orphanages, or setting up noodle factories inside the country. Our evaluations have revealed obstacles or risks that we've concluded do not line up with our objectives. We still do not know what the final picture will look like and continue to pray patiently and wait for God's clear signal before venturing into North Korea.

Ideally, we would want a high-ranking Chinese official or entity to partner with us to establish our language school within North Korea, which would protect our assets and workers while allowing us a long-term presence.

My Family

Following God's *mahashaba* (blueprint) for our lives has led me and my family through dark valleys and to stunning heights. God has used every event, difficult or delightful, for His purposes.

Our daughter, Jeanna, who had gone astray for a time during her youth, has found treasure in following God's blueprint for her life. She is devoted to leading worship at New Life as well as pursuing her passion as a bilingual teacher at an elementary school in Houston.

Our son, Timothy, is married and attends law school in Ft. Worth, Texas.

When we commit to living according to God's blueprint for our lives, we can be confident that our

Lord is always faithful to watch over us and guide us. Being a pastor and the wife of a pastor has its ups and downs, and life has a tendency to throw us off balance occasionally. At times we've had to grapple with betrayals, disappointments, and doubts, but Sue and I pledged many years ago to pursue the *mahashaba* God designed for us—no matter how that played out. As a result, our path has become clearly defined, and consequently we have become content with whatever God has for us. We are grateful and humbled that He called us for His purpose.

If I had sat down to create an amazing story to wow you and convince you of the truth of God's *mahashaba*, in my wildest dreams I wouldn't have been able to concoct such a tale: A brave Korean woman bears a boy conceived by an American GI and then suffers the Korean war and all sorts of adversity to protect this bullied and ridiculed half-Korean, half-American child. This boy will one day meet the famous Pearl S. Buck, come to the United States, and suffer uncountable trials that bring him to his knees before the King of kings. And this young man, unlikely to amount to anything, has the incredible privilege of establishing churches and institutes in the United States, Cuba, Mexico, and China for the glory of the King.

Does that even sound possible? By human standards, a resounding no! But by God's, truly all things are possible.

Look at your life right now, where you are. Choose to surrender your dreams and your will to the Author of your *mahashaba*, and watch while He brings all the pieces of your blueprint into place and His plan unfolds. Remember the Holy Architect's words from Jeremiah 29:11: "'For I know the plans I have for you,' declares the LORD, 'plans to prosper you and not to harm you, plans to give you hope and a future.'"

This is just as true for you as it is for me.